If you have ever felt like you don't fit, like your personality or strong opinions are just too much for some people, you'll be encouraged by Blake's stories. God's love for you is perfect, even when following Jesus doesn't feel easy!

CANDACE CAMERON BURE, actress, producer, *New York Times* bestselling author

In *Confessions of a Crappy Christian*, my friend Blake Guichet shares insights that will help you see the beautiful truth that God's love and grace are the only currency you need—because in Christ you are enough. Let go of trying to rely on your own strength, your own power, and your own wisdom by truly understanding the freedom Jesus purchased for you. This book is power-packed with stories, biblical insights, and practical applications on how to quiet the voice of fear and live out a free and fulfilled life.

RASHAWN COPELAND, founder and CEO of Blessed Media, author of *Start Where You Are*

In a world where many Christians sugarcoat (or completely avoid) the real and hard conversations, this book is refreshing. Unafraid to go there, Blake candidly guides you through honest conversations on everything from healing to sex, and she shares stories, thoughts, and biblical insights in both a digestible and thought-provoking way. If you're looking for a voice that tackles the tough stuff . . . you've just found it.

JORDAN LEE DOOLEY, *Wall Street Journal* bestselling author of *Own Your Everyday*

This is THE book! With poetic precision, Blake dismantles all the ways hustle culture gets it wrong. Her words are a needed breath of fresh air in a world attempting to suffocate us with illusion and quick fixes. Her transparency and honesty are the balm we need.

BETHNY RICKS, speaker and faith-based leadership expert

In a world of homogenous writing, *Confessions of a Crappy Christian* breaks out with extraordinary humility and vibrant, evocative writing. Raw, at times anguished, and always honest, this book discusses life in all its messiness, with all its disappointments, but also celebrates its wonder and joy. Blake Guichet writes with the perfect mixture of grace and truth; she's a faithful and fun companion on the journey of being an imperfect believer serving a perfect God.

GARY THOMAS, author of *Sacred Marriage*

I'm so thankful for brave women who say the things that no one else will say. Blake is one of those women. I got sucked into this book the moment I started reading it. Blake's voice is fresh, real, bold, and so very needed. *Confessions of a Crappy Christian* will invite you to break free from the pressures of a polished and perfect Christian life and instead relax into God's goodness while enjoying being who He created you to be. You will laugh, cry, and let out a deep sigh of relief. You will feel lighter after reading it, and that's something we all need more of in our world.

CHRISTY WRIGHT, national bestselling author of *Business Boutique*, *Take Back Your Time*, and *Living True*

CONFESSIONS OF A CRAPPY CHRISTIAN

CONFESSIONS OF A CRAPPY CHRISTIAN

Real-life talk about all the things Christians aren't sure we're supposed to say— and why they matter to God

BLAKE GUICHET

TYNDALE
MOMENTUM®

A Tyndale nonfiction imprint

Visit Tyndale online at tyndale.com.

Visit Tyndale Momentum online at tyndalemomentum.com.

Visit Blake Guichet at https://crappychristianco.com.

Tyndale, Tyndale's quill logo, *Tyndale Momentum*, and the Tyndale Momentum logo are registered trademarks of Tyndale House Ministries. Tyndale Momentum is a nonfiction imprint of Tyndale House Publishers, Carol Stream, Illinois.

For information about special discounts for bulk purchases, please contact Tyndale House Publishers at csresponse@tyndale.com, or call 1-855-277-9400.

Library of Congress Cataloging-in-Publication Data
A catalog record for this book is available from the Library of Congress.

ISBN 978-1-4964-5704-2

Printed in the United States of America

28	27	26	25	24	23	22
7	6	5	4	3	2	1

To every person who has ever been
told they are too much or not enough
by the people who should have
protected and encouraged them.
To the women bound up by something
that should have set them free.
To the wild, brave, and free ones.
This book is for you.

CONTENTS

FOREWORD

I STILL REMEMBER when I found Blake Guichet (@thegirlnamed-blake) on Instagram. I was holed up in a hotel in Kansas City as I finished writing my own book. Possibly like you, I just stumbled upon her content when someone I follow shared one of her posts. That's one of the cool things about the internet, right?

I don't even remember the particular post, but I do remember that Blake was calling out "hustle culture" (which I love!), she was calling out bad theology (which is honorable!), and she was giving glory to God (yesss!).

And I thought, *This girl is one of my people.*

So I actually sent Blake a DM that day. And because she is cool and legit and understands the importance of relationship building on social media, she sent me a direct message back. And now, here we are a few years later, as RLFs (real-life friends). It's funny how God knows the people we need (and the books we need!) right when we need them.

I am convinced that Blake is one of those women whom *everyone* needs in their life. She is always in your corner. She's probably also someone you don't want to meet in a dark alley if you've wronged her or someone she loves. She loves Jesus and knows the Word of God. She's incredibly honest (and in today's world that is hard to come by).

I find myself shaking my head and whispering "yes!" at so many of the subjects Blake writes about on social media and in this book. She talks about the hard things. The areas a lot of us wish we had the guts to talk about.

And even if you disagree with her stance on a topic (which I do—I vehemently disagree with her on the hot topic of *Die Hard* being a Christmas movie—it is *not*), she will cause you to think. That in turn makes me dig deeper into why I believe what I believe. And isn't that a good thing either way?

From a personal standpoint, I've been going through a few years of God surrounding me with Enneagram 8s. (If you're one of those people who doesn't love the Enneagram, then just skip this paragraph.) As an Enneagram 3, I can often bend and go smaller and stay quiet in order to keep the peace and stay likable. And yet I can't step fully into who God has created me to be and simultaneously continue to fear what other people will think.

So cue Blake as yet another Enneagram 8 in my life (joining the ranks of my husband, my teenage daughter, and my mentor). I'm convinced God has surrounded me with these "gentle bulldozers" so I can get better at speaking truth with more boldness and clarity. Blake does this so well. She is the grown-up version of my fourteen-year-old daughter. And that gives me such hope when I think about the woman my girl will one day be.

Bold.

Passionate.

Sold out for truth.

Sure in her beliefs.

Confident in her calling.

Unafraid to speak her mind.

And unapologetic about who she is.

No matter your personality type, Blake will firmly but gently help you find your voice too.

Social media is a brutal place a lot of the time, especially when you're talking about hard topics and having honest conversations that, quite frankly, a lot of Christians are not comfortable with. I've watched Blake navigate that with such grace and integrity. I've watched with so much admiration as she has grown into her role as an online influencer. Sometimes the spotlight can bring out the worst in people and shine a light on one's shortcomings. But Blake absolutely sparkles. That's what I love about this book: She models how to acknowledge and engage thoughtfully with the uncomfortable questions so many of us have when it comes to understanding ourselves, our work, and our relationships.

Blake knows she is already enough without getting accolades on social media. I love that she doesn't portray her life as Pinterest-perfect because whose life actually is? I love that she is so free to be exactly who God made her to be. I love that she shares her anxieties and struggles because it gives the rest of us permission to share our own. I love that she will say out loud what most of us are afraid to. And I love that she is a cheerleader for laying down our hustle and picking up God's best for each of us. Her conviction of whom she is working for and why she is working for Him is always evident.

If you are someone who struggles to fit in, or struggles in general, or if you are someone whose life has turned out differently from what you envisioned . . . you will love this book. If you are someone who is an Enneagram 8 or, like me, you need other 8s to make you bolder . . . you are going to love this book. And you are going to love Blake. You are going to love how she shows you how to navigate life, both in real time and on the internet, without apology and without hustle. It really is a permission-granting book. Not that either you or I need "permission."

But I am convinced that God will bring people into our world at exactly the precise time to help us learn or see something that we need. I am convinced that God will often allow us to fight our own battles so that we are able to come back from the battlefield, lick our wounds, heal, and then build a ladder to let down for someone else. This book is Blake doing exactly that. It will encourage and inspire you to be and do exactly what God is asking of you.

Xoxo,
Jen

WHY I CHOSE A CRAPPY— NOT A CURATED—FAITH

Some people just want to fight. Bless them with a block.
#2 OF "MY BEST (UNSOLICITED)
INSTAGRAM ADVICE,"
JUNE 13, 2020

I'VE GAINED AN ONLINE FOLLOWING largely due to my penchant for rocking the boat. For saying what people are thinking but are often nervous to say out loud. I've always been one to speak my mind, so I gravitated to online platforms early.

Though I posted my first photo to the site a year before my wedding, Instagram was barely on the scene when I married my husband, Jeremy. We didn't even have a #wedding hashtag (although I know it would've been super witty if we had had one). By the time my babies entered the toddler phase, Instagram was beginning to form into what it looks like now—fewer heavy filters and no captions, more life and microblogs. As a child of the Xanga and LiveJournal days, I welcomed the opportunity to share my love of words with an internet audience and began filling my feed with images and honest takes on life as a young mom, wife, and Christian. I love the immediacy of the medium: You can post images and ideas almost as quickly as they come to you and begin culling through responses and questions minutes—sometimes seconds—later.

Yet the more time I spent online, the more I found that the same issues plaguing Christian women in the real world—isolation, insecurity, FOMO—were exacerbated by our ability to curate our lives so they looked perfect on the internet. My struggles with mental health, friendship, marriage, and mother-hood seemed nonexistent on Instagram, but I knew better. I was sure others were fighting the same battles I was; they just weren't talking about it. In an age when life is lived out in fifteen-second internet microcosms, we're drowning in other people's highlight reels. We spend our days comparing what we have and who we are with what plays across our screens.

> IN AN AGE WHEN LIFE IS LIVED OUT IN FIFTEEN-SECOND INTERNET MICROCOSMS, WE'RE DROWNING IN OTHER PEOPLE'S HIGHLIGHT REELS.

After a couple of years, I'd finally had my fill of picture-perfect Instagram Christianity, which went no deeper than the stilted conversations I remember from my days in church youth group. I craved a reckless-abandon kind of authenticity, and I knew it was what other people needed too. I kept digging, searching for someone who was show-ing up in the trenches, and I found a few individuals, but not many. Not nearly enough voices were speaking into what I knew to be an epidemic of loneliness. So I decided to create a space for honest conversations.

The first episode of the *Confessions of a Crappy Christian* podcast debuted on my thirtieth birthday, December 10, 2018—the begin-ning of the wildest ride of my life. Out of my need for solidarity and vulnerability, a community of fellow crappy Christians has grown into the thousands. These women (and a few men) desire to boast in their weakness so that God's power can show itself to be perfect through it. These are people who don't need the world to think they've got all their crap together, who are free and wild to be who God created them to be while chasing down who He wants them to be. They're okay with their shortcomings but not from a spirit of complacent acceptance. They live out that blend of the already and not yet, knowing our Father has given us everything we need for life and godliness (see 2 Peter 1:3) without trying to conform to some weird "perfect Christian" box some in the church have set before us as the only option.

That's why, in the very first episode of my podcast, I pointed to the passage that has become a touchstone for my life. It's Paul's reflection on God's response when Paul asked Him to remove some unidentified difficulty:

> Each time he said, "My grace is all you need. My power works best in weakness." So now I am glad to boast about my weaknesses, so that the power of Christ can work through me.
>
> 2 CORINTHIANS 12:9, NLT

That's really the crux of it, isn't it? Believing that grace is enough. Living from a foundational knowledge that grace is not only all you need, but also that it enables your weakness to be used for greatness and God's glory.

When the constraints of a curated life came crashing down, what I was left with was enough, even if I didn't always feel like it was. It came down to knowing I was okay. In all my mess, with all my flesh's proclivity for ridiculousness, God wanted me.

The world doesn't need more perfectly presentable Christians. It needs people who love Jesus and are willing to show up and say,

"I can't do anything on my own. There is nothing good in me apart from Christ, but with Him, I am unstoppable. With Him, I am more than enough and He empowers my every effort."

Through the chapters to come, my hope is to invite you into the Crappy Christian family. Maybe you picked up this book because the title intrigued you—the idea that a Christian would call herself crappy piqued your interest. Or maybe you already identify as a crappy Christian but the fact that someone else would say the same surprised you. Perhaps you've been burned by religion and the indignant righteousness of Jesus' followers but have never quite been successful at extraditing yourself from His love. Whatever the reason, my prayer is this: that when you finish this book, you will finally feel free. Free to be wild and brave and exactly who He made you to be without fear of failure or retribution.

As we journey together, I'll be inviting you to engage with some tough questions about your identity, relationships, and faith. I'll go first, wrestling with the powerful, yet often unspoken, messages from both the world and the church about how we should think and act. My hope is that by going first, I'm able to provide a safe space for you to address some of the sources of your anxieties and struggles, acknowledging that life is hard but God is good and loves you more than you can imagine.

The journey to living in freedom in Christ never ends. There are always more chains to be undone, lies to be eviscerated, and truths to be planted. I believe the Father walked me through the fire of living surrounded by lies so that I could come back with buckets of water for those still in the flames. That is my desire for this book, and for you. That you would be free from the bondage of religion, the burden of striving, the yoke of judgment, and the chains of fear.

All right. Let's go get free.

Chapter 1

WHAT AM I CHASING?

*If I find in myself a desire which
no experience in this world can satisfy,
the most probable explanation is
that I was made for another world.*

C. S. LEWIS

IT'S THE SPRING after the birth of my second child, and I'm seated in the balcony of a little hip theater nestled in the outskirts of Los Angeles. The music is so loud my ears are starting to ring, but that's nothing compared to the energy buzzing through the women around me. There's something almost palpable in the air. I haven't been able to identify it yet, but if I'm being completely honest, I'm not sure I like it. All in all, I'm just excited to be here, seated next to my best friend at the time and far away from the responsibilities and general lack of personal space that consume my day-to-day as a stay-at-home mom. I'm here for a change. I'm here to finally hit play on my life after pausing it to be a full-time wife, mother, and homemaker. This is going to be the game changer.

Then suddenly there she is. The woman I've traveled two thousand miles to see. The woman who is going to help me finally find my purpose, chase my goals, and teach me how to live out the more I was made for. I push aside the small doubts and weird vibes in my mental peripheral and focus, pen poised above the cute notebook I've brought to fill with wisdom and insider knowledge. Whoops! First, it's time to dance. And jump. This isn't exactly my gig, but I'm here for the full experience, so I do my best to join in.

"Is this balcony shaking?" I yell in my friend's ear as I move my arms along to Beyoncé's "Run the World (Girls)," refusing to jump because, yes, the balcony is definitely shaking. *It's okay, it's all part of the experience.* After a few more songs and micro panic attacks on my part, because *For real, this balcony is going to come off the wall from the weight of all this jumping and dancing,* it's time to get to business. The things I want are within my grasp, and this woman is going to give me everything I need to finally grab them.

It feels appropriate at this point to tell you what the "it" I wanted was so that you can understand why I was standing in that balcony mob in the first place. I had decided I wanted to be an influencer. Okay, wait, don't put the book down yet. I promise I'm going to redeem myself from that admission. But it's important that you know where my head was at this time. I wanted to be Instagram famous, even though at the time I had fewer than a thousand followers and no momentum to speak of. But I had set my sights on internet fame as the capital *G* GOAL of my life. My intentions were embarrassingly shallow, looking for attention and money to fill holes in my life they would never fill, and I was doing everything I could to achieve my objectives. I truly thought a certain number of followers and a set income stream would fulfill me. Heck, I'd flown all the way to LA desperately hoping to find the secrets. But I was also extraordinarily tired. By the time I landed at LAX, I was six months into chasing this particular dream, and I was losing steam. Nothing was happening. People weren't pouring into my Instagram, my phone wasn't lighting up with calls to speak to stadiums packed full of people, and the tricks and tips that the internet gurus shelled out weren't working. In fact, they made me feel kind of gross.

And that's how I end up here, in a theater in Los Angeles, confident that this conference is the one thing I've been missing. I am prepared to let the references to Beyoncé as "our Lord and Savior" slide no matter how much they make my stomach flip. I furiously take notes through keynote after keynote. I post impactful quotes to my thousand Instagram followers so they know I am in the presence of greatness and hopefully can glean a tiny bit of knowledge from the fountain I am drinking so deeply from.

It's minutes into day two and we're jumping up and down to Macklemore & Ryan Lewis's "Can't Hold Us," and I have reached max capacity on jumping and dancing—if for no other reason than because I seem to be the only woman on this balcony who can tell it's about to come straight off the wall (#generalizedanxiety-disorder). I walk out and down into the lobby. It's empty because I'm the only idiot willing to miss even a moment of what we've paid tons of money to witness in that room.

And for the first time since my feet hit California earth, I talk to God, hurriedly throwing up a prayer: *Something is off, and I don't know what it is, but I know You're the only person I can tell about it. Can You help me discern what to take home with me and what needs to stay right there on the stage? Help me know and hear what You have for me and what's not mine to pick up. Okay. Amen.*

I wait until it sounds like the jumping has stopped and walk back to my seat. After that moment, though, I take notes just a little bit less energetically. I don't share any more inspirational quotes to Instagram, and I actually skip a few keynotes in lieu of spending time with some of the incredible women I meet there, most of whom I discover have started to feel strange about the experience themselves. It takes time for me to pull it apart and figure out why I feel the way I do, but then it hits me like a Mack truck. Everything about this experience has been about the speaker on stage and me. We exist in a vacuum where no one else and nothing else matters, only what we want. And all that has done is added toxic fuel to the already impressively self-centered goal I am in California to chase: to make my name great.

The moment I handed my dreams and desires over to the hustle, I was instantly faced with how small my dreams were in comparison to what those ahead of me have accomplished, and so I felt forced to inflate my goals to match theirs. No longer would it be good enough to write a book, it would have to be a *New York Times* bestseller. I wouldn't be satisfied with simply growing my following, I would need to be making money too. And again, none of this is inherently wrong, but at the rate I am going, fulfillment and satisfaction are always going to be just outside my grasp, and I know it. And I find it is an exhausting, defeating place to be.

LOOK AT ME

I've always wanted my voice to be heard (which I don't think is a bad thing). Since I was young, I've had something to say and wanted people to care enough to hear it. I basically came out of the womb wordy and loud, never allowed to sit next to my friends in grade school because you could set your watch by my teacher having to scold me for talking during class. Even as a child I loved to debate, rarely meaning to be disrespectful, but always wanting to understand—a character trait I'm sure my parents loved seeing emerge in their mouthy ten-year-old.

I desired to be known and heard, to teach and equip, but somewhere along the way my God-given desires had gotten jacked up. I didn't want to speak up because I had something to say about Someone greater; I wanted to speak because I wanted people to look at me. It took a long time and a lot of undoing, but once it was finally enough to rest in who God is and who He says I am, the message came through loud and clear: *You're chasing the wrong thing.* I like how C. S. Lewis puts it in *Mere Christianity*:

> Creatures are not born with desires unless satisfaction
> for those desires exists. A baby feels hunger: well, there
> is such a thing as food. A duckling wants to swim: well,
> there is such a thing as water. Men feel sexual desire:
> well, there is such a thing as sex. If I find in myself a
> desire which no experience in this world can satisfy, the
> most probable explanation is that I was made for another
> world. If none of my earthly pleasures satisfy it, that does
> not prove that the universe is a fraud. Probably earthly
> pleasures were never meant to satisfy it, but only to
> arouse it, to suggest the real thing.[1]

Neither earthly nor heavenly desires are immoral. In fact, I would venture to say God created us with them. We desire food because we are hungry. We crave sleep because we are tired. And we desire to be known and loved because God created us that way. He knows His presence, grace, and love are the only things that will ever meet our emotional needs because He put them there. The problem begins when we attempt to fit round, worldly pegs into the square, God-shaped hole inside of us. We think what we're chasing will give us what we so desperately want. As a result, we abandon the simplest, most beautiful answer: that God created humans with an ingrained need to feel known in order to draw us near to Him. Our desires aren't bad; it's what we pursue to quell them that can get us into trouble.

This tends to manifest differently in everyone, which makes sense since He created us so uniquely. Even though the answer to our longing is the same for all of us, how we search it out in the world can look very diverse. So your desire to be known maybe doesn't show up in your life the same way it has in mine. Maybe you don't resonate with a cross-country trip to LA chasing down fame.

It could be that you need close relationships to be seen and heard on an intimate level. It could be that you're asking too much of the people around you, hoping their love and attention will quiet your longing. Or you hop from friendship to friendship, viewing people as disposable—when you've gotten everything you can out of them, they're of no use to you anymore. Relationships are difficult because you're trying to use them to fill something no human, even at their best, will ever be capable of. Because you aren't convinced God *really* loves you, you are on the hunt for people who will. Relational intimacy isn't wrong, but if you think you have to chase after it, it won't ever satisfy.

Perhaps your need shows up as a desire to be recognized for your work and abilities. What you bring to the table proves your worth, and dang it, you *bought* this table and everyone is going to know it. Promotions and accolades are like crack to your hustling spirit, each *atta girl* like placing a flimsy Band-Aid over a screaming wound. If you're not working, then you're falling behind; rest is for the weak, and you won't stop until you reach the highest peak, and if you're being honest, it's most ideal if you're climbing it alone. You may long to hear God say, "Well done, good and faithful servant," but secretly you're afraid you'll finish the race, only to find out He's disappointed in you. If you run after being seen and known for your accomplishments instead of resting in the assurance that you are seen and known by the Creator, you're chasing the wrong thing.

Maybe you just need to feel okay. Safe, special, good enough, supported—all you want is to feel secure. You may temporarily find satisfaction in your job, family, friends, food, or working out. Maybe you discover a certain creative talent or natural ability to serve others, which momentarily fills the void and makes you feel fulfilled. But you know it won't last, so the hunt begins again, on to the next thing. You want so badly for God to show up in your life in a way you can feel and understand since He seems to do it for others, but never you.

Pick your poison. Chances are you know what you're chasing in hopes of fulfilling your deep, inherent need to be seen, known, and loved. Every single thing I did—every thought I had, every move I made—in that hustling season of my life, was an attempt to obtain and position myself as optimally for my benefit as possible. Obviously, that's super gross to admit out loud, but I think if we're honest, we all have a little bit of hustle culture in us. Maybe you're not quite as immersed as I was, or maybe you're drowning in it. But that God-created desire to be known and loved, the one intended to draw us near to Him so that He can abundantly and exceedingly pour out His goodness on us—that is the world's hunting ground. It preys on our God-given proclivities and exploits them for its gain. What the world has to offer is attractive. It's also smart. It hones in on whatever we think we lack, whatever we're chasing, and promises to fill in the gaps—something only God can do.

So there I sit (or stand, when the music is cranking) in the balcony, lonely and pursuing connection. The hustle tells me this is where I'll find my lifelong friends—here within the economy of work. It's a girl gang, and there's someone in this room who can help get me and every other attendee wherever we're going! "Just look around! I promise there is a person here who fits your exact business needs, who can give you what you're looking for." (These are real things I heard at that Los Angeles conference; I wish I were fabricating.) The hustle guarantees that if I just follow this exact formula (only three installments of $117!), I'll be more productive than ever before. It promises to teach me how to be the best, dominate sales, and climb the ladder of success. ("Oh, you don't have a job? It's time to get a side hustle.")

And those in the theater who came desiring fame are told that is within reach too. The message we hear is this: "You belong on this stage right next to the presenters, don't you know? And yes, being up here will provide everything you've ever wanted. It's time to stop apologizing for your ambition and get after it, girl!" We buy the books, attend the conferences, and make the "connections"—all in the name of self-betterment and growth, but in reality, we're hoping for so much more. And the hustle is telling you and me that it holds the key.

> THAT GOD-CREATED DESIRE TO BE KNOWN AND LOVED, THE ONE INTENDED TO DRAW US NEAR TO HIM SO THAT HE CAN ABUNDANTLY AND EXCEEDINGLY POUR OUT HIS GOODNESS ON US—THAT IS THE WORLD'S HUNTING GROUND.

The problem is that the most successful lies always have a little bit of truth to them. You and I know that there isn't anything wrong with desiring connection or productivity. That God has no problem elevating the voices of those who will proclaim His name. But it's in that often-subtle shift that things go sideways. At first glance, the Pinterest perfect quotes and formulas seem fine. *You're right, other peoples' opinions of me* don't *matter,* we tell ourselves, fingering the pages of the newest guru's book. *I am enough. I was made for more.* Slowly and stealthily, the rally cries of the hustle integrate into our everyday thinking, quietly eliminating the truth in those thoughts—other people's opinions don't matter because of what Christ says about us. We're enough because God made us enough. The more we were made for is Him.

But because there's a little bit of truth in there, we forget why we started this journey in the first place. Our need to be known isn't satisfied; if anything, it's intensified. Because now that we're in the hustle's grip, what we're continually being told is that there's more than this pitiful, measly life we're living. Even though it lured us in with promises of fulfillment and enough-ness and success, the bar keeps moving, always inches outside of our grasp. Many of us are bleeding out, be it emotionally, financially, or physically. We're doing our darnedest to crawl across the finish line someone else told us to cross, refusing to acknowledge that maybe, just maybe, we've bought a lie and none of this is what we were promised. We're putting paper patches on a hole only God can mend (the paper is really pretty though).

Meanwhile, the God of the universe—the One who created neutrons and the aurora borealis and Brad Pitt—He's just waiting for you and me to come to Him. He knows He can satisfy every need we have. I imagine it grieves Him to watch His children chase acceptance by running into the arms of the world in the same way it pains us to see our kids make choices we know aren't good for them. We were made to be known by Him and in that completeness behave like beloved children who need nothing this side of heaven.

So there has to be a way to do this right. There has to be a path on which we can live out our days satisfied in Christ while acknowledging that we'll be faced with earthly desires that we can satisfy as well. I think finding that path starts by honestly answering the question, *What are you chasing?* Close your eyes, take a deep breath, and ask yourself, *What am I running after; what is the number one thing?* Are you pursuing recognition? Comfort and safety? Numbers, titles, dollars? I'm not suggesting that honoring Christ and living in close connection with Him isn't in there somewhere because I'd venture a guess that it is. But is it *the* thing? Because if it's not, you've gotten it twisted, just as I did. You've already opened yourself up to distraction and derailment. Now here's the best news ever: There is no checklist to getting back to God being the main thing. There's no 12-step program, no waiting period, no scripted speech to recite. It's a simple shifting of our gaze.

> THERE IS NO CHECKLIST TO GETTING BACK TO GOD BEING THE MAIN THING. IT'S A SIMPLE SHIFTING OF OUR GAZE.

LOOK UP

We've already been forgiven and called righteous, given everything we need for life and godliness (see 2 Peter 1:3). All He asks is that we live like it. And the reality is that we'll need to lay our motives and pursuits at the foot of the cross every day until the moment He calls us home. Our flesh wants to be the most important thing, but the new heart God has given us knows and desires to honor our Lord and keep Him first. It's easy, at this point in the conversation, to wax poetic about keeping the eyes of our heart set on Jesus. While I agree with that sentiment, I'm a girl who needs something to hold on to, something real and tangible that I can practice to help me keep Him the main thing. Just in case you like lists and tangibility as much as I do, I offer three questions I ask myself to keep my motives in check and ensure that God remains the most important thing I chase after:

Whose glory am I working for?

For from him and through him and to him are all things.
To him be the glory forever. Amen.

ROMANS 11:36

The most efficient way for the enemy to deter you and me from doing the Father's work is to take good things and make them distractions. Your job, family, passions, and gifts are good things from God, through God, and for God—just don't miss that last part and make them for your glory. If you're doing the things God has put before you in order to make your own name great, you will start trying to do them out of your own power and find yourself always chasing after the next best thing.

I find it relatively simple to discern if I'm working for my own glory or for God's; it just takes a moment of introspection and brutal honesty with myself. Am I doing this because it's going to make me look good, elevate my name, and line my pockets, or am I doing it because it's the next right thing God is calling me to do to further the Kingdom and make disciples? Being honest about whose glory you're working for is the perfect recipe for quelling pride and striving because working for His Kingdom is the only thing that will ever satisfy.

Which of my relationships are most important to me?

Don't store up for yourselves treasures on earth, where moth and rust destroy and where thieves break in and steal. But store up for yourselves treasures in heaven, where neither moth nor rust destroys, and where thieves don't break in and steal. For where your treasure is, there your heart will be also.

MATTHEW 6:19-21

Okay, traditionally these verses are used around money and material possessions, but when thinking of relationships, I think it hits just as hard, maybe harder, for those of us for whom people hold much more weight than things do. I'm going to keep driving this point home—your close relationships are not bad. Your desire to have close relationships isn't something to be ashamed of. But are you more focused on storing up friendships and feeling loved by others than you are on furthering the Kingdom of God? Do you talk to your best friends about things before you talk to God about them? (Woof, self-imposed conviction on that one.) I have many a time been guilty of trying to squeeze life out of those around me, only to find myself exhausted and the other person disappointed. God is the only One who can fill those gaps for connection; everyone else is bonus.

How am I using my time?

Pay careful attention, then, to how you walk—not as unwise people but as wise—making the most of the time, because the days are evil. So don't be foolish, but understand what the Lord's will is.

EPHESIANS 5:15-17

Paul was so intense, sometimes it makes me laugh. "The days are evil"? Dude, calm down. But then you take a look around and think, *Maybe Paul wasn't as intense as I thought he was.* Our time on earth is precious and numbered, and while it may sound like Paul is giving the biblical version of a YOLO here, I think he's less telling us to make the most of our days (not bad advice) and more reminding us to seize every opportunity to tell people about Jesus and glorify Him with our lives.

That's not to say that we can't rest, relax, or do things that are just plain fun. You're never going to find me telling you that you have to keep your nose in the Bible, have worship music playing, or volunteer at your church every moment. Each is a good use of your time, but God gave us zip lines and sushi for a reason, you know? However, if you and I attempt to find life and happiness in fun activities rather than simply enjoying them as bounty of the Father's goodness, our motives are way out of balance.

Earth is God's playground, and I really believe He created it for His kids to enjoy. He designed us for relationships and community. He hardwired some of us with competitive natures to enjoy the thrill of business and entrepreneurship or athletic or musical endeavors. He gave some of us the gift of writing and speaking to share His message with the masses. He wants us to feel safe, secure, and accepted, but not by the world's definition—by His. All of these good things should drive us back to Him. Every single one. The methods and means may change, but at the end of the day, with clear eyes and full hearts (love you, Coach Taylor and *Friday Night Lights*), the drive behind what we do has to be only Jesus and His glory, all in hopes of drawing others to Christ so they can experience His love too.

That is the dream I want to chase. Understanding that, my friend, is the game changer.

Chapter 2

WHERE DO I GET MY WORTH?

If you don't know your own value, somebody will tell you your value,
and it'll be less than you're worth.

BERNARD HOPKINS

IF YOU HAVEN'T GATHERED BY NOW, I'm a bit of a go-getter. I've been this way as long as I can remember, like when I tried to sell rocks from my parents' gravel driveway instead of lemonade because, well, the rocks were right there. Or the time I read the entire Lord of the Rings trilogy as a ten-year-old simply because my teacher told me it would be too difficult of an undertaking. I'd organized more events, led more debates, and owned more businesses by the age of thirty-two than some people do in their lifetime. I'm overly energetic, which is why I've been completely caffeine-free for the last five years because it just puts me into complete and total overdrive. I like to get stuff done, and wasting time is the most surefire way to make me go crazy.

Right out of college I landed a pretty cushy job as an inside sales-person for a pipe-fitting company (yep, pipes). It was the furthest thing from my dream job, but it paid the rent and offered health benefits, so I took it, knowing it would be a stepping-stone to the right position. I don't think I lasted a full year before I moved into a management job at a local boutique. I worked there for about a year before taking a job managing a fitness center. I didn't last quite a year there before I decided it was time to go ahead and do my own thing. Clearly the traditional office job route was just not going to be my jam.

In the course of the next five years I opened a wedding planning company, coordinating upward of forty weddings a year—one when I was thirty-six weeks pregnant. When it became clear that having a husband with a demanding job and two little ones under two and a half wasn't jiving with working at a wedding every weekend, I transitioned the business into a graphic design firm. I started by working on wedding products and eventually moved into branding for small businesses. From the outside looking in, I was less traditionally busy because I wasn't out of the house four weekends a month, but in reality, I was busier than ever. I was designing and meeting with clients all hours of the day and night while trying to wrangle two kids and care for a home and a husband. All of that still wasn't "enough," so I added writing and Instagramming onto the ever-growing list of things I was working on. I launched a blog and began putting up multiple posts a week. I then began curating Instagram content with the hopes of growing a platform that might eventually provide some additional income and perhaps even bring along a book deal (I'd wanted to write a book since I was a little girl). Right around this point in my ever-changing work situation, things started to go a little wonky. Not only were my motives completely off-kilter, my definitions were as well.

Hard work and *hustle* are often considered synonymous, but in actuality they are nearly opposites of each other. In fact, back then I just assumed hustling meant you were working really hard. I was also pretty sure the Bible talked about working hard in a couple of places so like . . . we're good, right? Except no, we very much were not.

I think it's important to differentiate the two from the get-go, and while I thought about using Webster's traditional definitions of the two terms, the more I looked at them, the more I realized they lacked the lived experience that fleshes them out and distinguishes them from one another. So how about some good, old-fashioned, lived-in, Crappy Christian definitions?

THE HUSTLE

Get up and grind.
Go get what you want.
Work while they rest.
It doesn't matter if you get tired, keep going.
Don't take no for an answer.
You are the hero in your story.

Do any of those statements sound familiar? That may be because every single one was pulled off a different cute little graphic I found on Pinterest. These are real-life mantras that people embrace and live out every single day. I should know. As I previously mentioned, when my younger daughter was three months old, I opened a graphic design company. The lack of things to do was making me crazy (heaven forbid I just snuggle a new baby), so I up and launched an entire business by myself. I've heard from friends since then that it just looked like I was a new mom who had it all together and was creating an empire with a baby on her hip, but allow me to pull the curtain back for you. What it actually looked like was mountains of undone laundry, weeks of takeout for dinner, snapping at my husband constantly, ignoring my then three-year-old, and feeling completely insane. All for the sake of feeling like I was killing it and contributing when I was, in fact, drowning. I needed to feel purposeful and fulfilled to the max capacity possible, so I just kept piling things onto my plate until it was spilling off the sides and onto others.

That is the hustle, friend—one of the most self-centric ways to live. It's exhausting and demanding and never stops because if it did, you might fail. And failure is death. The hustle requires everything of you and will never, ever let you believe that a no or a closed door could be the best thing to happen to you. The hustle puts it all on your shoulders. It makes you assume that other people are unreliable because they're likely out to get what you've worked for. You were born to pull yourself up by your bootstraps no matter what lot life has handed you. At the end of the day, the hustle is all about you and what you can accomplish. It doesn't matter if you're tired, your health is failing, or you haven't played with your kids in a week. It's always demanding: Are you getting out there and getting what you want?

The hustle views others as expendable or transactional, something to be gained or used in the pursuit of success. It sells you a membership into a girl gang, but what you usually end up with is a bunch of cutthroat women out to make a dollar or climb the ladder. The community aspect is severely lacking because most people in the hustle just straight up do not know how to view others as anything other than their competition (we'll get into this more later). Imagine forty women trying to pull a rope in forty different directions during a tug-of-war competition because each thinks the way she is pulling is most important. That's what it feels like to be in the hustle.

I'll never forget what that frenetic, anxious energy felt like when I was consumed by hustle culture. It came with the understanding that if I didn't treat this dream like it was the most important thing, then no one would and it would fail. And if it failed, I failed. And if I failed, what was the point of going on? It took a literal crash and burn to free me from its chains. It took sitting in a doctor's office while an endocrinologist looked at my blood work, looked at me, and then looked back at the papers before half-whispering, "I don't know how you're sitting upright right now."

My cortisol levels were off the charts, and my vitamin D and B levels were nonexistent. I was in full-blown adrenal failure, and the prescribed treatment, other than a few steroid and vitamin injections, was rest. My doctor told me I had to chill out, and at that point I knew I had no other options. I was waking up tired and could barely keep my eyes open long enough to drop my preschooler off for car pool. I was always hungry, clumps of hair were falling out in the shower, and I often had to sit down because of light-headedness. I had worked my body into the ground. This was my wake-up call.

Every part of my life was touched by my obsession with hustling and succeeding, down to how I approached my normal day-to-day—something I'm still working today to undo. In fact, I recently found myself lying on my couch for days on end due to a particularly rough bout of anxiety and panic attacks. A few days in I realized I had been attempting to create a list of things I had "accomplished" that day in order to make myself feel better about my current state and immediately sat up and said out loud, "Oh, *gracious*!" I had fallen back into the brainwashed mindset that what I did dictated how good or okay I was, even on one of the hardest days I'd had in a long time. And that, in my opinion, perfectly sums up the control the hustle has over someone caught up in it.

HARD WORK

When I first started speaking out about hustle culture, I got a fair share of pushback from people who were still within its walls. I got DMs on Instagram telling me that I was anti-woman, that I didn't want women to be successful—which if you know me is humorous. A lot of the negative feedback I got felt . . . personal. As if people felt like I was coming for them directly when I spoke up about hustle culture. I suspect they resented that I was openly threatening the false god of success, and—oo boy—people don't like it when you come for their idols. (I speak from personal experience.) When your identity is wrapped up in what you do and how well you do it, it's uncomfortable to have someone come poking their nose into your business, telling you that stuff will never complete you. I'm a big believer that freedom is often on the other side of what makes us uncomfortable, but I also get that this message can feel threatening to those who've built their lives around the messaging of the hustle.

> FREEDOM IS OFTEN ON THE OTHER SIDE OF WHAT MAKES US UNCOMFORTABLE.

I also got a lot of sincerely confused questions about what the opposite of hustle is. Are we just meant to coast? Are all side hustles sinful? How do we do this right?

Well, lucky for us, Scripture is jam-packed with verses about the glory to be found in being a diligent and fruitful worker:

Commit your actions to the LORD,
    and your plans will succeed.
PROVERBS 16:3, NLT

Let your good deeds shine out for all to see, so that everyone will praise your heavenly Father.
MATTHEW 5:16, NLT

Remember the words of the Lord Jesus: "It is more
blessed to give than to receive."

ACTS 20:35, NLT

Use your hands for good hard work, and then give
generously to others in need.

EPHESIANS 4:28, NLT

Work with enthusiasm, as though you were working for
the Lord rather than for people.

EPHESIANS 6:7, NLT

Make it your goal to live a quiet life, minding your
own business and working with your hands, just as we
instructed you before. Then people who are not believers
will respect the way you live, and you will not need to
depend on others.

I THESSALONIANS 4:11-12, NLT

In fact, many passages are pretty ruthless toward those who
are unwilling to carry their weight and work alongside others.[1]
When I began to come off the high of the hustle, I really needed
those verses. I needed to know that my natural desire to work
diligently wasn't "wrong" or sinful. I knew it would require a
personality exorcism for me to not be an entrepreneurial-minded
individual who was always striving to be the hardest worker in
the room. These Scriptures taught me that hard work is biblical
and showed me how to follow God's guidelines for diligent work
rather than try to keep up with the hustle's demands. Another
one of my favorites comes from Paul's letter to the church in
Colossae:

> Whatever you do, do it from the heart, as something
> done for the Lord and not for people, knowing that you
> will receive the reward of an inheritance from the Lord.
> You serve the Lord Christ.
>
> COLOSSIANS 3:23-24

"Do it from the heart." This sounds like something a coach would say in a cheesy high school football movie when the team is on the three-yard line and six points behind: "Do it from your heart. Leave everything you've got on the field. Go out there and show them how it's done." That's what I imagine Paul's mindset was as he was writing these words to the church in Colossae: *Whatever you do, just make sure you do it all the way because you're working for God, not man.* There aren't any qualifiers here. It's not "when you're at your office job," or "when you have a super important employer." No, whatever you do, whether that's wiping butts or writing books, it all matters, and it always matters that you're working from your heart.

> Unless the LORD builds a house, its builders labor over
> it in vain; unless the LORD watches over a city, the
> watchman stays alert in vain. In vain you get up early and
> stay up late, working hard to have enough food—yes, he
> gives sleep to the one he loves.
>
> PSALM 127:1-2

When your heart is positioned toward the hustle, everything depends on you, how hard you work, and how well you can get it done. When you work hard for the Lord, you get to work from a place of resting in and relying on God.

Hearing no sucks. It doesn't matter if the no comes from someone you know, from a stranger, or from God. It's difficult to hear no from the time we're kids all the way into adulthood when that simple, one-syllable word can make us feel as if all our dreams have been dashed. But I'll be honest, some of the hardest noes I've ever gotten turned out to be the sweetest gifts from God. Like the boy I thought I was going to marry who broke my heart. I'm convinced that I probably would be divorced by now if that had been a yes from God. Or all the noes I've heard in my business and creative endeavors: "You're not a good fit," "You need to grow your platform more," and on and on.

The most stressful, high-stakes meeting I ever had ended up in a no I thought would be a yes. A popular Christian celebrity's representation contacted my representation (just kidding—that's me; I don't have "people") to set up a meeting about possibly acquiring my podcast for their network. This would have been huge for me personally and for my business as I had just left a podcast network and my team and I were in the midst of figuring out what the production side of things would look like. I thought surely this was God dropping a way out into my lap, so we prayed and prepared for the meeting. Our talk went okay, but I could tell right off the bat that we weren't as good of a fit as I thought we were. And sure enough, we never heard back from the network. But here's the thing—I tend to work better alone. I don't like being told what to do or how to do it, so even though the partnership would have provided great exposure and experience, the God who created me with a strong independent streak knew His girl had no business being in a podcast network. I needed to strike out on my own. So I did. And that no turned into a really sweet gift from God. At the time of the meeting, I had no idea what the future of my platforms was going to look like, no idea the things God was going to call me into and ask me to use my voice to speak about. And I know with certainty that had that no been a yes, I would've been muzzled in some capacity. Striking out on my own, albeit sometimes harder and scarier, also allows me to (mostly) speak freely and unfettered as the Father leads.

Every no stings, but because the Lord is the one building my house, I am able to accept and embrace each one like a welcome friend. What God has for me is better. I've met people who are completely wrapped up in building their own proverbial houses, nose to the grindstone. They never take no for an answer when it would mean giving up on what they want. And it's all in vain, according to the Lord. Is it not so much better to labor under the direction and blessing of the Father, allowing Him to lead your path, than to waste your life and energy working against His plans?

EMPTY OR ENERGIZED?

Come to me, all of you who are weary and burdened, and I will give you rest. Take up my yoke and learn from me, because I am lowly and humble in heart, and you will find rest for your souls. For my yoke is easy and my burden is light.

MATTHEW 11:28-30

I know, I know. You've heard this one a million times, but stay with me because these are some of the most marvelous words a go-getter can read. First of all, can we talk about the fact that Jesus calls us to Himself? Like, whoa. That's huge. And He doesn't just call us; He invites us to exchange our self-sufficiency for His rest. His terminology would have made sense to the farmers and toilers who likely were listening as Jesus described His yoke as easy and light. Back then animals were yoked together, often two at a time, to bear the burden of pulling equipment. Just as they shared the burden, so Jesus' yoke is easy and the burden is light because He carries it with us. We were never meant to do it all of our own volition, and we certainly were never intended to drudge it out until the task is completed. We were created to rest in the glory of Jesus' finished work, both literally and figuratively, and to work hard alongside our Lord, allowing Him to empower our best efforts.

> Let us not get tired of doing good, for we will reap at the proper time if we don't give up. Therefore, as we have opportunity, let us work for the good of all, especially for those who belong to the household of faith.
>
> GALATIANS 6:9-10

One of the hardest parts of being an entrepreneur (or having that proclivity) is that it can naturally be isolating and self-focused. It's just the nature of it, but that doesn't mean we have to shoulder the load alone. My favorite way of differentiating the hustle from hard work is found in the admonition tucked into Galatians 9:10: "Let us work for the good of all." In other words, we can ask ourselves, *Who benefits from our hard work? Is it only us, or is our work in the best interest of everyone it touches?*

Our natural tendency, of course, is to hustle harder to ensure that number one is taken care of. But Scripture makes it easy to step into the unburdened, free way of working and out from under the reign of the hustle by reminding us that we can work for the Kingdom of God in every facet of life. That can be as simple as trading in a self-focused mentality for the opportunity to bless others with our hard work. It may show up as saying no to good things for the sake of our mental and physical health. Or holding our dreams and desires with open hands before the Lord so He can do what He will with them.

HOW TO SPOT (AND LIVE OUT) THE DIFFERENCE

I had to unlearn a lot of practices when I came out of hustle culture. I've had to set obnoxiously strict work boundaries for myself because otherwise I will sit in front of my computer from the second my eyes open in the morning until I collapse from exhaustion at the end of the day. I know this about myself and have forced myself to be honest, not only with God, but with those in my life who can tangibly hold me accountable. I've been forced to let incredible opportunities and collaborations pass me by because I knew my mental health, my body, or my family wouldn't hold up under the stress required to pull them off. One or more of them would pay the price. I've had to absorb the sting of hurtful noes to my dreams and really put in the work to practice what I preach by believing that God is just as much in the no as He is in the yes. But most of all I've had to let the Lord build the house. Not only build it, but own it. I've had to unclench my fists that held my dreams and ambitions so tightly so I could offer them up to the Lord. And you know what? He's blown my mind every single time.

Over the years He's taken my sometimes-reluctant obedience and just straight up shown off. He's done things far beyond even my wildest dreams, and I'm a wild dreamer. He's opened doors I never could have opened, built bridges I would otherwise have burned, and redeemed pieces of me I believed to have died a long time ago. All because I shifted my outlook from *This is my house and I'll build it how I want* to *All right, God, let's do this together. It's all Yours anyway.*

That's the kind of working relationship I want you to have with your Father. For your own sake, I invite you to loosen your grip on your dreams and hustle habit. Hold them with open hands so that when the noes (and the yeses) come, they're free to flow through your fingers. Stop working so dang hard all the time and enjoy the life God has given you! What's the point in being wildly successful if you never enjoy it? Put boundaries up around the precious parts of your life and don't allow anything to leap over them. Refuse to buy into the lie of competition and jealousy, and be stubborn in your pursuit of community and friendship within your working life. Believe the best in others, believe the best in yourself, and openhand-edly welcome others, including God, into your journey.

Just in case you need to hear it, remember that you and God are on the same team! He wants far better things for you than you want for yourself.

ARE YOU WORKING HARD OR HUSTLING?

If you are tired and burned out in the pursuit of whatever you're going after, I invite you to ask yourself some questions.

Whose glory are you working for? (Yep, there is that question again.)
What's the motivation behind what you're building?
And are you working for Jesus and His Kingdom or for glory on earth?

If the answers point back to yourself, you may have the heart of a hustler who loves Jesus, but your motives have gotten off-kilter somewhere along the way. The good news is this: All it takes to get back on track is to fix your eyes on Him until the answer to all three questions is simply *Jesus*.

Chapter 3

CAN GOD REALLY USE MY WEAKNESSES?

Grace carried me here, and by grace I'll carry on.

UNKNOWN

WHEN I STARTED WRITING THIS BOOK, I polled my Instagram audience about what they wished more Christians would talk about. Overwhelmingly, two answers came in on top: sex and the issues over which Christians struggle in silence and in the dark. Things like money, jealousy, pride, broken friendships, disordered priorities—you know, the light and fluffy stuff!

I've done my best to include as much sex talk in this book as can be viewed appropriate, but when I saw the second topic, I immediately put my phone down and said, "No, thank you," out loud. I don't know anyone who enjoys talking about the ways they personally struggle to measure up, what they're not great at, their sin struggles. It's uncomfortable and revealing, and our survival instincts tell us not to expose our weaknesses because that will make it even easier for our enemies to take the kill shot—or maybe that's just me. (Of course, now that you've read about how I once danced the hustle, you know I finally got over my reluctance to talk about personal struggles.)

Because of our human nature, we want to be perceived as strong and capable rather than weak and inadequate. We want others to know we can carry our own weight; we don't want to be known for the burdens weighing us down. So we keep our weaknesses, sins, and shortcomings in the dark corners, unseen and talked about only in hushed voices and only when we are so desperate that we need to discuss the monster in the closet.

From an early age, we are taught, whether subliminally or deliberately, that weakness is bad and undesirable. We need to fight extra hard to avoid being seen as weak, especially if we're a member of the "weaker" sex. Therefore, when faced with our own frailty, we simply do not know what to do with it.

I learned this lesson early—the day my mom dropped off seven-year-old me at summer camp for the first time. Hand in hand we walked up the gravel path to Camp Old Hickory, a wonderland of horseback riding, archery, and kayaking. My older friends had told me stories of their adventures there, and I had been talking about going to Camp Old Hickory for years, all hyped up about the experience.

A few steps from the entrance, I let go of my mom's hand, walked to the edge of the path, and threw up. When I was done, I walked back over to her and simply said, "I'm kind of nervous."

My mom still sounds shocked when she tells the story years later. On the outside, I had just seemed excited. She had no idea that on the inside my stomach was doing backflips due to anxiety and the fear of being away from my parents and in a new environment.

If we're being honest, we all have a little bit of that seven-year-old in us—trying to hold our own frailty inside or hiding it behind our backs, hoping no one else sees the parts of us we just can't seem to get right. We pray and ask God to take them away or make us better. Sometimes He does because that's His way. And sometimes He doesn't because that's His way too. He's good either way, and we can be fine either way too. That's because the Christian life is not one marked by having it all together, but instead by serving the One who does.

> THE CHRISTIAN LIFE IS NOT ONE MARKED BY HAVING IT ALL TOGETHER, BUT INSTEAD BY SERVING THE ONE WHO DOES.

The topic of weakness is nuanced for the believer. We know that we've been made right in the eyes of God and that we've been given a spirit of power, love, and self-control (see 2 Timothy 1:7), but we also know we are human. Until we reach heaven, our human bodies and natures will war with the new hearts God has given us. The result: weakness and sin. We do the very things we hate even though we have been made new in Christ. After all, weakness kind of begets sin, doesn't it? In order for sin to be present in our lives, we have to have been weak enough to let it in.

I've noticed that we often put Christian leaders on a pedestal and are astonished when they fall right off it onto their faces. Whenever a prominent pastor's private sin is made public, we are shocked; after all, we've convinced ourselves that there's no way someone that close with God could possibly fall because of weakness or sin. This could be, in part, due to our own tendency to place people on pedestals they never asked to be on. But I think our desire to keep the hard things hidden is a major reason we've assumed that "strong Christians" don't struggle.

I don't know if you're allowed to prefer one Bible character over another or if you're supposed to love them all equally the way God does, but I do have favorites, and one of them is Paul. To be fair, the guy wrote about a third of the New Testament so he's kind of an easy pick, but I resonate most with how Paul presents the gospel and his shoot-'em-straight communication style. There's a lot about Paul's life that I can't necessarily relate to; for instance, I've never been shipwrecked and (shockingly) never been in prison.[1] But what I love about Paul is that he doesn't try to pretend that his life and walk have been something they're not. Many of us, on the other hand, spend much of our lives attempting to clean things up, to make them more presentable or more easily consumable—be it our experiences, our feelings about those experiences, or our own personal struggles. We don't want to be or feel like a burden to others, so we shut them out of the difficult stuff. We can't stand the thought of being defined by the things that are hard for us, so we don't allow them to be a part of the equation at all.

Paul does none of that. He lays it all out there, keeping a running list of the terrible things he's walked through but continually pointing back to the goodness of God. He also never lets the reader forget that he was once the worst accuser and persecutor of Christians, but he always praises God for his radical transformation. Paul seems to have mastered the balancing act of acknowledging the bad while praising God for the good. His approach is no different when it comes to acknowledging his own weakness:

> In order to keep me from becoming conceited, I was given a thorn in my flesh, a messenger of Satan, to torment me. Three times I pleaded with the Lord to take it away from me. But he said to me, "My grace is sufficient for you, for my power is made perfect in weakness." Therefore I will boast all the more gladly about my weaknesses, so that Christ's power may rest on

me. That is why, for Christ's sake, I delight in weaknesses,
in insults, in hardships, in persecutions, in difficulties.
For when I am weak, then I am strong.

2 CORINTHIANS 12:7-10, NIV

These verses come directly after Paul has shared a magnificent
vision with the people of Corinth. As always, Paul just lays it out
there—admitting he could fall prey to pride just like the next guy,
as if he were thinking, *Yeah, that vision was great and so to keep me
from getting too big for my britches, I was given a thorn in my side.*

There's a lot of debate over what this thorn in Paul's side was.
Some say it was a physical ailment; others a sin or temptation. But
whatever it was, I think it's important to note that the root word
Paul used for *thorn* in this passage characterizes a tent stake, not
a thumbtack.[2] Paul's problem wasn't a mild irritation or something he dealt with only sometimes. It was a mega-issue in his life,
something that afflicted and frustrated him often, maybe even
constantly. He explained that he was not above struggle and weakness but that God enabled him to delight in those weaknesses for
the sake of being made strong.

I want to make sure this is clear: Every single person you know
who loves Jesus has weaknesses. That person who comes to mind
when you think "good Christian" is not exempt from the battle
with flesh. Every pastor you listen to on Sundays has areas of life
in which they have to guard extra heavily against the pull of sin.
The authors of every book you've read struggle and battle against
their own thorns in the side. Present company included.

Since I was young, I've had a pretty tough exterior. I was bullied
quite a bit in elementary school; as a nonconformist since birth, I
had no interest in doing the things kids my age typically did. Third
grade was the era of peer-formed "clubs," and I wasn't invited to

any of them. While my classmates ran around on the playground, I enjoyed the cool AC on hot Louisiana afternoons and read Nancy Drew mysteries and *Anne of Green Gables*. When everyone else lined up for soccer tryouts, I spent my evenings in my grandmother's ballet studio. While everyone else was singing NSYNC, I learned all the words to every Garth Brooks song. I even had a weird name, a boy's name for all accounts and purposes. I was different, and not in a cool way.

Those younger, formative years didn't exactly cultivate a natural penchant for trusting people my age. And so, to match my Teenage Mutant Ninja Turtles sheets, I formed a shell. I assumed people would find things to poke me about—exterior issues such as what I liked to do or read or listen to were up for public evaluation and opinion, but gone were the days when people would willy-nilly have access to me. As the years passed, however, the shell transformed into walls, and the walls became a fortress. And then I built a moat around that fortress. And the bridge to cross the moat and gain entrance to the fortress continually got narrower. For a long time, I was quite comfortable in the fortress. I had no real need for friendship or connection outside of my few close friends, the ones who already had access to my armory.

A coping mechanism I'd developed as a way to get through the school day had hardened. Brick by brick my pain had built a fortress around my heart so isolated that some days I didn't even want God inside. I could shrug off my detachment as the natural result of being a lone ranger or "not needing people as much," but the truth was that I was wounded, walking with a limp, and using pride and isolation as crutches.

And then someone I'd allowed into the walls set the fortress on fire, exposing my hurt and insecurities to others. As devastated as I was, we serve a God who wastes nothing, even our pain. Ever so gently, as I sat amongst the ashes of the walls that had kept me safe for so many years, He whispered, "They needed to come down anyway."

By the time my fortress was set ablaze, I was mostly incapable of real relationship since that requires trust and opening up with another, and I had absolutely no desire to do either. The hurt and pain of childhood had created wounds that now crippled me as an adult. Something would have to change if I was ever to experience the connection to others we were created for. So standing in front of a wall of my own burned-out building, I started picking up bricks and handing them to God. That looked like starting therapy, where slowly but surely, I unpacked my issues with the anger, pride, shame, and fear that stemmed from childhood bullying. I recognized my natural proclivity to keep people at arm's length, not because I didn't need friends but because I was deathly afraid of ever giving someone the opportunity to hurt me again. And I began to acknowledge that some of what had been said about me had made a home in my heart as truth. *Maybe I really am just a nerd with no friends. Maybe being different is a bad thing.*

I went through a long, honestly painful process of unearthing things I'd spent my whole life keeping in the dark. But once my counselor and I had dug up the garbage, we started replacing it with truth. Truth about who God is and who He says I am. Truth about vulnerability, authenticity, and relationship. For too long I had taken pride in being a well-educated individual who didn't really need many friends. Someone who could trounce everyone at trivia night but who didn't have many friends to go there with. I was replacing the lies by which I had chosen to define myself with a true identity in Christ and nothing else.

The process was daunting and overwhelming. Some days I didn't want to do the necessary reconstruction. But God stayed with me and I stayed with it, and over time, my heart softened and my pride was replaced with humility. I learned that I do, in fact, need other people because God has gifted and equipped other people in ways I am deficient. He taught me that there are people worth trusting, and that sometimes when trust is broken, it can be rebuilt. And He showed me that vulnerability is a superpower, one that He can take and use far beyond anything we can imagine.

So now, like Paul, I do my best to boast in my weakness because my penchant for pride and walls remains. There's no point in pretending that I've dragged them all to the junkyard and left them there. Instead, I'm like a child sneaking bricks and lining them up in a row. When confronted about that, I have a ready excuse: "I just wanted to see what they look like! I'm not actually building a new wall!"

Yet daily God asks me to lay down my pride and allow people to see inside and love me well. Daily I have to kill the part of me that wants to straight-arm into oblivion anyone who approaches me. I would have preferred if God had simply taken away all the ashes of my former fortress, all the pain of my childhood, all the memories that drove me to build those walls. But what He gave me instead—strength—is better.

When you carry a burden, someone can offer you relief in one of two ways—either by taking away the burden or by strengthening the shoulders the burden sits on. And that's what God's grace and Jesus' sacrifice do. They strengthen our shoulders so that we can continue to bear our burden in a way that glorifies the Father (more on this soon). Considering my background, there is absolutely no way I could let people in if it weren't for His constant bolstering of my spirit. There is no explanation for my ability to show up vulnerably and authentically, other than the grace of God. Grace for me and for them and for you. Grace is the favor and love of God in action, not only withholding what we deserve, but giving us what we don't. I've learned through experiencing God's grace how to give grace to myself. I've found that when I let His grace in, I see myself differently—less through my own eyes and through His a little more. I remember that He likes me and loves me and didn't make a mistake when He made me. That He sees and recognizes my pain and how I got where I am but that He loves me too much to let me stay there. His grace is available all the time. It doesn't run out, I don't monopolize it, I am never outside its reach. It's always available, even when I might not want it.

God's grace makes a difference in every aspect of our lives, but especially in our weaknesses. It removes the shame and guilt—the unvarnished *ew-hide-it-away-ness*—and instead gives us one more reason to point to the Father and tell others "It's all Him." I think some of us believe that Christian maturity exists in a vacuum outside God, as if once we've arrived, we need Him less. This, however, is the furthest thing from the truth. Only when we remain completely dependent on the Father and His grace will we continue to grow in righteousness.

In the end, Paul was literally advertising the thorn in his side. He wasn't resigned to it or putting up with it or still hoping it would disappear. That thorn was now worth boasting about because it was one more way he was able to point to God and say, "His power and glory, not mine." I'm sure Paul arrived at this place a little more quickly than present company did, but I can tell you he's right. It's better on the other side where you're neither ashamed of your weaknesses nor convinced that they're not weaknesses at all. The place where you know that God meant what He said when He told you His burden is light and His yoke is easy (see Matthew 11:30).

Jesus didn't mean life isn't hard. He just meant He'd be in it with us. And no fortress offers greater security and protection than that.

Chapter 4

WHAT DO I DO WHEN MY DREAMS ARE DASHED?

Hope is being able to see that there is light
despite all of the darkness.
DESMOND TUTU

IN THE "NATURE VERSUS NURTURE" DEBATE, I am a case study for those who say nature is paramount. Loud, opinionated, always up for a debate (or argument), I am an anomaly in my household. A megaphone amongst whispers, I am jokingly asked by my family where I came from. And I've always been this way, self-reliant and stubborn even as a young child. My mother has me to thank for many a gray hair. So it should come as no surprise that even though I'm the daughter of a gentle neonatal nurse practitioner and a devoted dance instructor, I decided I wanted to be a lawyer when I was very young.

As girls my age fantasized about being ballerinas and mommies, I daydreamed about monogrammed briefcases and finally getting my chance to holler "You can't handle the truth!" in true *A Few Good Men* style (why I knew that line from that movie, I still don't know). I took every civics, ethics, economics, and government class I could in high school. I participated in mock trials (and won them), and I spent my breaks hanging out with the long-tenured social studies teacher Mr. Byrd. He helped me discover my love of policy, as I flipped through his ancient governmental studies books and he patiently answered every question I had. When I was accepted at Louisiana State University, it was a no-brainer that I would be a political science major, and I thrived. I sat in front in every history class, and I was one of the only weirdos fully enjoying PS 101: American Government. These classes felt like the pinnacle of a long-awaited dream; I was actually making steps toward my long-held ambition to become a lawyer.

And then during the summer before my sophomore year of college, I fell in love with a cute, fratty, dynamic boy. He was only my second boyfriend. As to be expected, he had a dream of his own—to become a professional football coach. If you don't know the ins and outs of becoming a professional sports coach, trust me when I say it's an extremely competitive prospect. During our three years of dating, his dream was front and center in our relationship. I was so in love with this boy that even when our relationship turned toxic and unfaithfulness ravaged the trust we had built, even when I could feel my dream slipping through my fingers, I held on to him. By the start of my junior year, I sat in an academic adviser's office asking her to help me piece together a degree so I could just graduate. You see, the boy was a year older than me, so he would soon graduate and pursue coaching as a full-time gig. I had no time to go to law school if we were to stay together because there was a 99 percent chance he would have to move as he began his career. And obviously I would be going with him. So why even bother attempting to graduate with a political science degree if I was going to be a coach's wife?

My dream of a legal career—the one that had been slowly fading, replaced by the dream of the one I loved—evaporated in the academic adviser's office. Even though my boyfriend had already cheated on me once, breaking not only my heart but also my spirit, I was giving up my own dream so I could help him pursue his. By now I was a shell of the girl who had walked onto LSU's campus. But I was still in love, no matter how toxic that love had become, so I had decided sacrificing my dream was worth it.

Then, even as we were still dating, the boy fell in love with another girl and started dating her. And everything fell apart. I'll never forget how I felt while lying on a cold, crappy apartment bathroom floor trying not to throw up as I stared into space and realized what I had done.

There was no going to law school for me now. My scholarship had run out, and my parents had paid the part they had always promised to pay. The idea of being buried by student loans gave me the runs; I simply could not do it. And so in that moment, all I could feel was failure. I had failed the girl who dreamed of courtroom scenes and gavel-pounding drama. I had failed Mr. Byrd, the teacher who had invested uncountable hours pouring knowledge into my law-loving high school brain. I had failed my parents and wasted years, and now I was sure I was destined to be a failure for the rest of my life.

Looking back now, I know that the only failure would have been staying on that floor, letting the lies and fear and overwhelm keep me there. But when you're smack in the middle of a vortex of realization and devastation, it is quite difficult to perceive the positive ahead. It can be near impossible to say to yourself *Step one: Get off the floor* and consider that a victory.

The truth was that, in some ways, I *had* failed. I would never in good faith counsel another bright, smart, college-aged girl to put aside her dreams and aspirations to follow her already-unfaithful boyfriend around the country so he could teach other boys how to throw a ball. That would be foolish and pretty terrible advice. *Merriam-Webster* defines failure as "a lack of success,"[1] and yes—I had lacked success when it came to going to law school. I had failed, but I was not a failure.

I did eventually get off the bathroom floor and graduate from LSU. Shortly after that, I began dating my now husband. Because God really does waste nothing—even our "lack of success." That doesn't mean the process isn't going to suck; that there aren't going to be moments like the one on the bathroom floor when you cry out and ask God why. But it does mean that, if we allow Him in, He won't waste any of those moments of defeat.

As an idealistic college freshman, I thought the best plan for my life was very simple but intense: I would graduate, go to law school, obtain a prestigious job with a firm out of the state (preferably somewhere with a subway system), establish myself as an incredible lawyer, and then maybe by the time I was thirty-five find time to marry and pop out 2.0 kids. It took a while for me to stop white-knuckling that agenda and accept that God's best plan was so much better. In His version, I met the love of my life three weeks after the person I thought was the love of my life broke my heart. No wonder it took time for me to realize that was what was happening. Jeremy likes to tell people I actually tried to break up with him a few months into our relationship because things were *too good*. He was too good to me, our relationship was too easy, and I thought that couldn't be right. Surely after I had thrown a bomb on my life plans, things couldn't be this good. But they could, and I would go on to marry him eighteen months later. We had our first child a year after that. Then I eventually pieced together a job in online ministry that consists of podcasting, writing, and educating.

Thankfully, the very same gifts that I thought made me cut out to be a killer lawyer have lent themselves to this surprise career. The tenacity and drive for justice that drove me as a young person continue to fuel my efforts as an adult in a career I never planned for.

I know that not everyone finds themselves in a beauty-from-ashes situation immediately after things go horribly wrong, and I've been there too. Sometimes we trudge through hardship that seems to overlap with more hardship, wondering when it will end and what the point of it all is. Today, my struggle is with anxiety. I can't tell you how many times I've asked God to take it, changed medications, tried a new coping mechanism—all in hopes that this hard thing would just evaporate. And it doesn't. I'll be honest, I still have days when I don't understand why I've been given this thing to carry that serves no purpose. But I do have faith that God won't waste my struggle.

The life I thought I wanted wasn't the life I was meant to live. That doesn't mean it was easy to let go of. Even today when I'm reading through congressional bills to share a deep dive on Instagram, twinges of regret pop up, reminding me of what could have been. I'm not where I thought I'd be. But I know, without question or pause, that I'm exactly where I'm meant to be, that God's best yes was a no. And I know I'm only able to hold that attitude because of who God is.

> I'M NOT WHERE I THOUGHT I'D BE, BUT I KNOW, WITHOUT QUESTION OR PAUSE, THAT I'M EXACTLY WHERE I'M MEANT TO BE.

A quick flip through Scripture is all it takes to encounter story after story of characters whose lives didn't go the way they planned, often because of the choices they made. I'm sure Adam thought he'd live the entirety of his life in Eden, but his sin expelled him from the Garden. I doubt Noah expected to be known as the guy who built the huge boat and survived the water apocalypse, but because of his faithfulness, he saved all living things from extermination, allowing the human race to begin again. Sarah probably thought she'd be a mom before she turned ninety, but in the end, she birthed a patriarch of Israel at that advanced age. By now we've made it only to Genesis 21.

My personal favorite story of a life gone not-the-way-planned is Moses. From his birth, Moses' story is one of twists and turns, beginning with him floating down the Nile so he wouldn't be part of the mass slaughter of Israelite boys occurring at the time. Well into his adulthood, Moses was directed to paths he not only didn't expect but didn't want.

Though he was spared the slavery endured by his fellow Hebrews, one rash decision forced him to flee to the desert, where he wandered as an obscure shepherd for four decades. Then one day, God appeared to him in a burning bush, drastically changing the trajectory of his life. After the Lord gave him his assignment, Moses protested: "No, LORD, don't send me. I have never been a good speaker, and I haven't become one since you began to speak to me. I am a poor speaker, slow and hesitant" (Exodus 4:10, GNT). I've lost count of the number of times I've responded to life's curveballs with the same sentiment. Convinced I've taken a wrong turn and something is amiss, I cry out: "This is all wrong, Lord. I'm not the one; this isn't the right path; I can't do this." Because when things don't go according to our plans, we're inclined to decide they're not going according to His either. And so, in our humanity, we tell Him so. Whether it's because of our own decisions or a sharp left turn into uncharted territory, we find ourselves begging God, "Don't send me." And in His unending kindness and grace, He answers us just as He did Moses thousands of years ago: "Who gives man his mouth? Who makes him deaf or dumb? Who gives him sight or makes him blind? It is I, the LORD. Now, go! I will help you to speak, and I will tell you what to say" (Exodus 4:11-12, GNT).

Moses is just one of numerous people we meet in the Bible who thought they were on a road leading one place when, in fact, it led to another, whether they got on that road by choice or chance. Some end up on unexpected roads via the choices they made, like Jonah ending up in the belly of a whale. God told him to do one thing, he disobeyed and did another, and—*boom!*—he became fish food before finally traveling to Nineveh, the plan the whole time. The lives of some people changed in a flash because God made it so, like Saul's quick flip from persecutor of Christians to apostle of Christ (now going by the name Paul). I bet if you'd asked him when he was going around having Christians stoned or beheaded if he'd ever be one of them, he would have . . . had you beheaded. And yet we have most of the New Testament Epistles because Paul wrote them. Scripture is full of stories of people whose lives took drastic changes, all for the glory of the Father and steeped in hope in Him.

Like many of them, we initially resist His redirection. When I was paralyzed by fear, fully understanding that my own choices had led me to an unexpected foreign land, the cry of my heart was *No, Lord. Don't send me into the unknown. Don't let things go this way.* I thought I needed Him to do a magic trick and miraculously change my school records. I didn't know what I was going to do, how I was going to do it, or even what the next step was. It wasn't the last time I would feel this way either. I've whispered, "No, Lord, don't send me," more times than I can count, trying to avoid difficult situations, hard conversations, and controversial topics. And each time, the Father kindly responds, *Who put you where you are? Who made you who you are? Who has measured each step and is never surprised? It is I, the Lord. Now go, and I will not only guide your way, but empower your efforts.*

We spend so much of our lives trying to tell the Potter how to form us (see Isaiah 45:9-11) that we miss out on the opportunity to be the clay. After a lifetime of being hardheaded and sure I was right—after years of trying my hardest to be the Potter—I've learned that I'd much rather be the clay. The Potter not only knows exactly how He plans to form the clay, He knows what shelf He will set it on and whether it will be used as a vase for flowers or a mug for coffee. And while the clay has the job of doing what it was made for, it can do so believing and trusting that the Potter made it correctly so it can fulfill its purpose. Of course, that's all fine and dandy when we're sitting comfortably on a shelf, happily doing what the Potter created us to do, but what about when we're convinced He used the wrong mold when creating us?

One of the most popular "Things just got bad; I need comfort" verses is Jeremiah 29:11: "'For I know the plans I have for you,' declares the LORD, 'plans to prosper you and not to harm you, plans to give you hope and a future'" (NIV). A quick read of this passage can certainly feel like balm to the soul, a sweet reminder that God's got you now and has good things for you in the future so it's all going to be okay. And that's true. God does have you now and in the future, no matter what your path looks like or what you thought it would look like—even when it doesn't feel like He's got you. When everything was crumbling around me as I realized I would not be going to law school, God still had plans to prosper me and not to harm me, even though my circumstances didn't necessarily show it. Even when I felt as if my life was at a dead end, even when I didn't understand what God was doing or why He was doing it, He really did still have plans to prosper me. And if I had read these verses then (I honestly may have), I would've been sweetly reminded of that. But as with any place and time in Scripture, there's more to the story—more context that brings this verse to life, giving it a deeper and even more powerful application to our lives.

Jeremiah spoke these words over Hebrews who centuries before had lived under Egypt's rule and now were captives and exiles in the Babylonian empire. They were smack in the middle of some dark, heavy, despairing times, living under the domination of their enemies, who forced them to move from their homeland to a foreign country.

Just before Jeremiah's declaration, another prophet named Hananiah assured the people that God told him He would break the yoke of dominion and they would return to their homeland within two years (see Jeremiah 28:1-4). There was just one problem: God hadn't told Hananiah that; Hananiah was a false prophet sharing alluring news in order to draw people to him.

Sound familiar? Often, in the midst of our despair, in the middle of our hardest days, people will tell us that God said it's all going to be rainbows and butterflies . . . ASAP. I really believe they have good intentions, but it's still dangerous to tell others that God told you something simply to make them feel better. Because God doesn't promise immediate rescue. There will be times in life that don't make sense, times when we've taken a turn straight into the desert instead of the promised land. And in those seasons we can be tempted to believe the charming words of those who say that God promised it would all be easy and idyllic. We can assume that if we were just living "inside" the will of God, things would be easier, not so hard. But do you want to know God's will for our lives? It is for us to love Him and love others. His will isn't to provide us with some dome we live underneath, one we can duck outside of and then back into so we'll always be safe. God does cover the entirety of our lives in His love, yet still—life happens. Life is an accumulation of experiences—some beautiful and some difficult—and maybe, just maybe, they're all within His will because we live in His grace through them all.

It's important in our difficult seasons to remember what God actually promises the Hebrews in Jeremiah: They won't be traveling an easy road, but it's one He's paved for them. There is purpose in hardship, in the not-being-where-you-thought-you-would-be, because affliction produces endurance and endurance produces character and character produces hope (see Romans 5:3-4).

Not perfect hope, not hope without struggle, not hope without doubt. God doesn't ask us to muscle up hope that never wavers. Hope is a person and that person is Jesus, and all He asks is that we keep our eyes on Him even when the seas get rough and the path gets rocky. There were days after my breakup when hope felt just outside my grasp. I felt sure God or I had messed up my story. I assumed that I, the clay, could somehow jump out of the Potter's hands and wreck the whole reason for my being. But God. But hope. Hope carried me through the unknown and the confusing, from crying in the darkness to being able to see the light at the end of the tunnel. From the bathroom floor to fully embracing the life God knew was better for me.

> YOU SERVE A GOD WHO WASTES NOTHING, ISN'T SURPRISED BY ANYTHING, AND USES EVERYTHING—EVEN YOUR LESS THAN STELLAR DECISIONS.

You are not hopeless and neither is this season (or the one you just came out of or the one you're going into). You serve a God who wastes nothing, isn't surprised by anything, and uses everything—even your less than stellar decisions. The moments that feel like the end of the road are often just the

WHAT DO I DO WHEN MY DREAMS ARE DASHED?

beginning of another. Your future really is upheld by the same Father who promised to prosper and give the Hebrews hope.

Would I have been a great lawyer? Probably. But would I be living the full, to the brim, beautiful life I'm living today? I don't know. I'm not supposed to know. I'm supposed to rest in the confidence that the Potter knows what He's doing, and that's enough.

Chapter 5

SHOULD I FOLLOW MY FEELINGS OR THE TRUTH?

*Sometimes, telling your brain to erase what
your heart has written is hard, but I know someday,
these two will complement each other.*

IJEOMA UNEGBU

BEING A HUMAN IS HARD. I think we can all agree on that. It's less difficult when we get to do it with Jesus, but the truth is He never promised it would be easy. Yes, seasons come and go and bring struggles and victories with them, but for me, it's often the inner turmoil that's hardest to live with—the warring within myself between the truth and my emotions, what's actually happening and how I feel about it, the desire to stay rooted in reality but not smash my feelings down inside. It seems like I'm constantly asking myself things like *Is my husband being short and snippy with me, or am I hungry or tired or being overly sensitive? Did that person mean to hurt my feelings with their words or actions, or are old wounds resurfacing?* And that's not to say I'm always mature enough to ask myself those questions. Living in a broken world that isn't your home is rough. Between politics and viruses and riots and shutdowns, there's been enough hardship over the past few years to cover a decade. And that's just the headliner stuff everyone's talking about.

The Earth has continued to spin; life has gone on. Bills need to be paid, children reared, and marriages protected. We still need to deal with our personal crap, which has been compounded by what's happening on our doorsteps. Needless to say, there's a lot of room for feelings. And I'm going to say this multiple times throughout this chapter: Feelings are not bad. God saw fit to create us with varying degrees of emotions and feelings: ways to process our circumstances and experiences and connect us to one another. Emotions aren't immoral or dangerous, but letting them run the show can be. And if we live and base our beliefs about others and God only by what we feel, completely ignoring the truth He's given us, we will be in trouble faster than you can say *pneumonoultramicroscopicsilicovolcanoconiosis.* (If you ever want to impress your friends, tell them that's the technical medical term for a lung disease caused by the inhalation of minute silica particles. I'm honestly shocked we didn't see *that* disease reemerge in 2020.)

It's possible to take this too far in the other direction and process our experiences only from facts. You know the type; people who point to black-and-white terms and negate very valid emotional responses to both God and life. I like to call this the "new wave of pharisaical living." Such people may have their theology correct, but their approach to life is wrong. They crush others under the weight of doctrinal facts, seeming to almost take pleasure in watching others stagger under the burden of living life by a set of rules (see how Jesus describes them in Matthew 23:4). We're going to do a deep dive on the emergence of Instagram Pharisees in a later chapter, but I bring them up here as an example of how *not* to do feelings. Both emotional extremes handle feelings badly, either by letting feelings run the show or by removing them from the stage completely.

God created feelings and facts to live in tandem. Emotions have helped humans evolve and survive. They inform our decisions, initiate our fight-or-flight response, and allow us to connect to other people. But when we enter into a life with Christ, we learn to actively take our thoughts captive and put them under the authority of Scripture and believe that what Christ tells us is true (rather than what the world tells us; see 2 Corinthians 10:5). We get to walk through life not only having accepted Jesus, but living rooted in the Lord (see Colossians 2:7). If we don't, we can build a narrative in which the world is crashing down around us or a loved one has turned against us and we're completely alone in life—all by letting our feelings take the place of facts.

As I've grown older, I've become less emotional and more analytical, but oh boy, in my younger years, feelings took center stage, the lead part, *and* understudy. The whole kit and caboodle. Everything I did and said was informed by the feelings raging within me with little to no thought to the consequences or collateral damage they would cause. I spent three out of four of my undergraduate years in an impressively unhealthy romantic relationship—breaking up and getting back together with a boy I was bound and determined to marry (good lookin' out on that one, God). And because I had no capacity to take my thoughts captive and no interest in being rooted in the God I knew and said I trusted, I was a walking disaster.

One of our more epic breakups occurred at my not-birthday party well into our dating relationship. Yes, it was as cute as it sounds. Standing on the back porch at a party he had planned on my birthday but not for my birthday, said boy casually mentioned he wasn't sure he wanted to date me anymore. He then walked back into the not-birthday party. It's been over ten years, and I can still remember the way my head started spinning in that moment. Everything I thought I knew came crashing down around me, and because feelings trumped facts back then, I had nothing solid to grab on to. I physically had to sit down so my knees didn't give out.

Eventually my friends found me and took me home because your girl was losing it. Sure, some of that could be attributed to years in a toxic and borderline abusive relationship that would unfortunately continue on, even after the breakup at the worst birthday party ever, but looking back on her now, I mostly just see a girl who didn't know the truth. I see a girl who had not yet learned to allow her emotions and truth to live in harmony but instead allowed herself to be thrashed around by whatever the emotional flavor of the day was. Because here's the thing about living by feelings: When things are good, they're *g-o-o-d*. Sometimes I think that facts and truth aren't quite as necessary when life is pleasant and the water is smooth. When your boyfriend likes you and life feels steady, you feel steady because your reality is being informed by what you feel. And what you feel is good.

It's when everything goes south and you haven't spent any time rooting yourself in truth that the wheels come off. Your feelings hop in the driver's seat while facts are tied up in the back seat struggling to get loose so they can help drive the car, which is what they're there for.

If I could rewind eleven years and relive the birthday breakup, it would go so differently. For one thing, I like to think I wouldn't be in that position in the first place because if you're going to plan a party on my birthday but not for my birthday, I'm thinking maybe I should take the hint (okay, I promise not to harp on the party anymore). But if I could only go back to that one microcosm of a moment as the woman I am today, less emotionally driven but still in touch with my feelings, I suspect it would have been less devastating. Would I have been able to absorb what he was saying and obviously be very emotionally impacted by it but not rocked to my core? Would that moment have been the final straw it likely should have been, enabling me to walk away and save myself even more heartbreak? Would I have cried out to God instead of crumbling to the ground? If I had known the truth, would I have been able to preach truth to myself?

Because if I had, I could have reminded myself that my worth will never come from a person (see Galatians 1:10). I could've intimately known that my Father was near in that painful, difficult moment (see Psalm 34:18). I likely would have been able to preach truth to myself, that I am worthy of loving and loving well (see Luke 12:6-7). And that approach would have been the perfect collaborative work of feelings and facts. I would have acknowledged my feelings as well as the truth revealed in Scripture that grounds my worth in the God who created me, gave Himself for me, and loves me. There's no need to be cold or distant, completely removed from the emotional facets of life, but you can see from my experience the danger that can follow being exclusively informed by the feels.

Of course, sometimes we're on the receiving end of ire coming from a person driven by their feelings. One of the most difficult experiences I've ever endured is when someone chose how they felt in a moment over the truth of who I had proven myself to be. Maybe you've never driven eight hours with multiple kids in tow to support a friend's big accomplishment only to end up having the friendship go up in flames because you forgot to pack your meds and weren't at your best. I'd venture a guess, however, that you have a similar story of a relationship ending because someone chose to hold on to a moment in time rather than remember the truth.

In my case my feelings got hurt and I walled myself off (lack of serotonin to my brain definitely didn't help). But even after the fact,

I found that my singular lackluster moment had infected my friend's view of our relationship until the friend I'd spent the most time and energy loving and championing was telling me she didn't feel like I supported her *at all*. I felt like I was living in an alternate reality. Yes, I had been wrong to wall myself off and allow old wounds to cause bad behavior on my part. But in the end, our friendship could not survive this new reality in which I'd been cast in the role of villain when I knew I was not. She'd forgotten who I had been as a friend for years and allowed her feelings to become the capital *T* truth. I felt as if she buckled those feelings into the driver's seat and sent them barreling right toward me. Ultimately I just had to move myself out of the way.

Here's what happens when we live exclusively from feelings: We cease to think critically. We stop testing our conclusions and start assuming whatever we feel is most important. For example: David hurts Alexis's feelings with a sharp and biting comment in a moment when he is personally struggling. In that hurt, Alexis has a choice to make. She can either assimilate herself with the wrongdoing and contract friendship amnesia—wiping her memory of all the times David has been there for her, shown up, pushed through difficult seasons, and loved her well. Or she can preach truth to herself. She can grant herself the time and space to feel what she needs to feel while simultaneously acknowledging that David is who he has always been, human and flawed but still a great friend. Likely you've played both roles in this exercise: the wronged and the one who wronged another. Left with a choice to make, do you light a match and burn it all down because of the way you feel, or do you allow truth to permeate pain? Personally, I've done both. Can you see the importance of preaching truth to yourself in your relationships?

Be honest: Have you ever felt like you and God are David and Alexis? You wouldn't be the first and won't be the last to feel this way.

Read Psalm 13 and you go on quite the roller-coaster ride with the biblical David as he laments his sense that God has forgotten him.

> How long, Lord? Will you forget me forever? How long will you hide your face from me? How long must I wrestle with my thoughts and day after day have sorrow in my heart? How long will my enemy triumph over me?
> PSALM 13:1-2, NIV

David's honesty is my favorite thing about him. The dude pulls no punches on how he feels about himself, others, and God. He lets himself feel what he needs to feel and cries out in the depth of the pain of abandonment. That can often be the first step in preaching truth to ourselves: We ask God to step in. Too often we attempt to navigate the minefield of life and feelings alone, believing God is too busy or the issue is too small to warrant His attention. Look, if God knows how many hairs you have on your head (see Luke 12:7), I'm thinking He also cares enough to step into your heartbreak and struggles. And when we cry out to God, He preaches truth back to us. Watch David do an emotional U-turn in Psalm 13, from "Why have you forsaken me?" to this: "But I trust in your unfailing love; my heart rejoices in your salvation. I will sing the Lord's praise, for he has been good to me" (verses 5-6, NIV).

Did you catch that? Literally two verses after David asks God where He is, he speaks of the Lord's unfailing love! You can think David's feelings are all over the place, or you can see this shift as the result of David preaching truth to himself. The truth from God's Word is that He never leaves us or forsakes us (see Hebrews 13:5). So while we may feel as though God has withdrawn His presence from us, the fact is that He's true to His word and He's sworn to never leave us.

We've covered our tendency to replace facts with feelings in the realm of our human relationships. But I think this tendency is most rampant (and dangerous) in our feelings toward God because this is the relationship that informs everything we do. Think about it—if you're walking with the Father through life, aiming to honor Him and introduce others to Him, everything you do flows out of that. Every earthly relationship, every one of your actions and reactions is an outpouring of who God is and who He says you are. And if you don't know the truth of who He is (read more in chapter 7)—if you think He's against you, that He doesn't want good things for you, that He thinks you're bad, etc.—you're on shaky ground, sister.

> THE BEST WAY TO CALIBRATE YOUR FACTS AND FEELINGS IS TO GROUND YOURSELF IN THE TRUTH OF GOD'S CHARACTER AS REVEALED IN SCRIPTURE.

In fact, the best way to calibrate your facts and feelings is to ground yourself in the truth of God's character as revealed in Scripture. From personal experience and what I hear from others, I believe three of the thoughts we battle most often when our feelings threaten to take the upper hand are: "God thinks I'm bad"; "God won't protect me"; and "God will love me only if I . . ." Let's see what the Bible tells us about each.

FEELINGS VS. FACTS, BIBLE EDITION
I feel like God thinks I'm bad.

You are a chosen race, a royal priesthood, a holy nation, a people for his own possession, that you may proclaim the excellencies of him who called you out of darkness into his marvelous light.

I PETER 2:9, ESV

In verse after verse, especially in the New Testament, God speaks to His kids about how He views them. Spoiler alert: It's all positive. Once you leave your old life behind and step into union with God, the old you is dead and the new you has been brought to life: "If anyone is in Christ, the new creation has come: The old has gone, the new is here!" (2 Corinthians 5:17, NIV).

Because of Jesus' finished work on the Cross, God sees His followers as perfect and holy. When we choose sin instead of the new heart God has transplanted into us, we go against who we really are, but that doesn't change how He views us. Honestly, if it was that easy to undo what has been done, why would He have even been willing to sacrifice His Son for us? That's the truth I always come back to with the "I'm depraved; I'm so awful" rhetoric. Those things were true about us before we were in Christ. If those sentiments stay true after the fact, does that mean our sin is more powerful than Jesus' blood? I haven't been able to find any evidence to back that up.

Before you entrusted God with your life, you were dead and your name was nowhere to be found in the Book of Life. God did not count you as His own but instead, as His enemy. ALL OF THAT CHANGED WHEN YOU ACCEPTED HIM. I apologize for yelling, but this is so important I want to make sure you get it. When you feel as though God thinks you're bad, you're believing a lie from the pit of hell intended to keep you from living in His abundance. And you're better than that. You are worth what God paid for you—the life of His Son, Jesus.

I feel like God won't protect me.

The one who lives under the protection of the Most High dwells in the shadow of the Almighty. I will say concerning the LORD, who is my refuge and my fortress, my God in whom I trust.

PSALM 91:1-2

When someone tells me they feel this way, my first question is always: "Protect you from what?" Because if you believe God won't shield you from hardship or loss, your feelings are actually correct. Nowhere in Scripture does the Father guarantee us an easy road. In fact, He basically promises the opposite—hatred, trials, temptation—the whole gang is there! Often when we walk through dark and difficult times, we believe that God has somehow failed us. That He hasn't held up His end of the bargain in ensuring a clear path before us. But in this case, we've gotten His promises all wrong. He promises to avenge us, which implies there will be things worthy of avenging (see Romans 12:19). He's committed to use our trials for our betterment, which means there will be trials to walk through (see Romans 8:28). But my favorite promise in times of trouble comes from Psalm 46:

> God is our refuge and strength, a very present help in trouble. Therefore we will not fear, even though the earth be removed, and though the mountains be carried into the midst of the sea; though its waters roar and be troubled. . . . God is in the midst of her, she shall not be moved; God shall help her, just at the break of dawn.
> PSALM 46:1-3, 5, NKJV

Our heavenly Father never said we wouldn't walk through deep waters, but He promised to be in them with us. He promised to provide refuge and comfort in the midst of trouble. The point of the Christian life was never for things to be easy and light, but for us to know that we never have to shoulder our burdens alone. So the next time you're struggling with feeling as though God isn't doing His part by protecting you from the crashing waves of life, ask yourself: *Am I seeking refuge in God, or am I expecting Him to act like a genie whenever I wish it all away?*

I feel like God will love me only if I complete this checklist.

For you are saved by grace through faith, and this is not from yourselves; it is God's gift—not from works, so that no one can boast. For we are his workmanship, created in Christ Jesus for good works, which God prepared ahead of time for us to do.

EPHESIANS 2:8-10

There's this great debate in the Christian world about our works. Do they matter? Are they important? Are they necessary for salvation? Personally, I have little time for grand theological debates. After all, there are souls at risk, and I find that connecting with them is more fun than talking with people who use only huge words that even after ten-plus years of being a Christian I can't understand. But there is one hill I will die on over and over, and it's this: There is nothing you and I can do to get into heaven outside of grace through faith. You can't checklist your name into the Book of Life. You can't perform yourself into God's Kingdom. Grace via trust. All that is required of you is faith.

I know that one sentence has just ruffled a whole bunch of feathers. But hear me out: I'm not saying that our good works don't matter or that there shouldn't be evidence of change in our lives when we became believers. But that's not what I'm talking about. I'm talking about God loving you. All that He requires is faith. Paul tells us in Romans 8:35-39 that nothing can separate us from God's love. As children of God we should be known by our fruit and the good works God prepared in advance for us to do (see Ephesians 2:10). Those things, however, do not define us or make us worthy of His love. We could never earn God's love, so Jesus died to secure it for us.

GRACE + TRUTH = SOLID GROUND

As you dig deeper into Scripture to combat the lies you tell yourself, I'm not asking you to function like an emotionless robot. In fact, please don't do that; you would be absolutely no fun. But I am going to lovingly challenge you to let God plus truth regain center stage. You don't need to be thrashed around by a world set on manipulating your feelings for its gain. You can love people for who they are and love yourself for who God made you. You can stand on the back porch of your crappy boyfriend's house and preach truth to yourself.

You can thrive in the generous grace God has given you, informed by your feelings but defined by the truth. And y'all, that is a beautiful thing to experience and to witness in others. Nothing beats the ability to take a deep breath when faced with a difficult task or situation and confidently say, "I acknowledge that this makes me feel {fill in the blank}, but I also know the truth is {fill in another blank}." That statement means you're reclaiming the power God gives you. Just hearing it makes me want to do an end of the Breakfast Club–style fist pump into a freeze-frame.

I want that confidence for you, and I believe God wants that for you as well. He wants our lives to be built upon the solid rock of His truth rather than the shifting sand of the world's. The best way to live that out is to saturate your life with His Word so that whenever you're faced with a challenge or a doubt, choosing God's facts over your feelings becomes the easiest part of your day.

Chapter 6

WHY DO I ALWAYS FEEL LIKE TOO MUCH OR NEVER ENOUGH?

I'm a woman phenomenally. Phenomenal woman, that's me.
MAYA ANGELOU

HERE'S THE TRUTH: I've gotten where I am today because of God's goodness and by functioning out of who He made me to be. Not by bending to the narrative of who the world thinks I should be. Not by subduing my natural gifts and personality traits under the suffocating instruction of certain teachers in the church. I'm here today, writing these words, because I've followed the Lord's leading in forging a path in the online Christian world. Less fluffy Christianese, more leaning in on the hard topics people are dying to talk about but too nervous to bring up. I didn't always see it this way; in fact I once asked my business mentor if she thought I should "water things down" to be more easily consumable. And I thank the Lord for strong women; her answer was an immediate and resounding no. "In fact," she told me, "I think you should double down." She was right, and I followed her advice. I stopped being afraid to share controversial opinions. I no longer felt as if I needed to follow the path laid out by earlier Christian influencers and authors and instead blazed my own. I quit tiptoeing around the things I knew the Lord wanted me to say online and dove in with faith that He would guide the way. And He did. Every single time.

You see, I don't look or sound like the traditional Christian woman—the one we were taught was desirable in Sunday school and in youth group. As I was growing up, the Proverbs 31 woman was presented as the pinnacle of Christian womanhood, the model we were all meant to strive after and look like. It would be years before I came to realize I'd never actually met the *true* Proverbs 31 woman. The woman I had been taught about was a distortion of who she really was, seen through the lens of chauvinism, legalism, and a complete misunderstanding of what women of God are capable of.

To be honest, I kind of despised that version of the Proverbs 31 woman, whom I pictured sitting at home knitting and serving her husband's every wish and whim. I wanted nothing to do with that or the image of the docile Christian woman as portrayed by the churches I grew up in.

I absolutely did want to be of noble character, and when I finally decided to settle down, heck yeah, I wanted my husband to consider me worth more than gemstones. But in the meantime, I didn't have time to select wool and flax and make linen garments (see verse 13). I just couldn't believe God created women to shuffle around doing their husband's bidding, never speaking up, never having a thought or pastime of their own.

I was taught that the Proverbs 31 woman was the poster child, the perfect example of biblical servitude and submission. The thing is, there's some truth there. Yes, women are definitely called to be service-hearted and submissive, but too many teachers who emphasize these characteristics water the Proverbs 31 woman down until she is nothing more than an errand runner, a house-keeper, and a seamstress. But she is so much more. Not only that, but the apostle Paul actually calls men to an even higher level of service and submission in Ephesians 5:25-26.

In my opinion I was the furthest thing from the Proverbs 31 woman—or at least the version I was introduced to at church. As a result I spent years praying God would change me. I felt God's will would be to make me quieter and meeker, to make my words land more gently, and to soften the pitch of my voice so it didn't always rise above everyone else's. This was the version of a godly woman I heard about. So much of my life was spent questioning how God created me rather than walking in it. I'm not quiet or docile, and I ask lots of questions, especially of those in authority. I'm a natural leader, go-getter, and boat rocker.

In fact, my youth leaders and camp counselors lost me at the very start: "Who can find a virtuous wife? For her worth is far above rubies" (Proverbs 31:10, NKJV). All through adolescence and high school, I was completely and unequivocally uninterested in being someone's wife. In fact, my adversity to marriage was so well known that my younger sister bet my father that I wouldn't get married until I was thirty. After all, my sister knew I had dreams and aspirations: I was going to law school and would become the greatest female criminal prosecutor the world had ever seen.

And then two months before my twenty-third birthday, my sister had to hand over fifty dollars to my dad when I married the love of my whole life. Obviously, something had changed, and as dreamy and wonderful as my husband was (and is), it was more than just meeting him that changed the trajectory of my life. I had figured out that the way Christian womanhood is sometimes unpacked from pulpits is crap.

When I took the time to study Proverbs 31 for myself, I realized that her account has often been twisted and watered down by Christian leaders, so far from the woman of action and leadership she actually was. Likewise, I stopped feeling like a rebel for being the woman of Christ I was and finally recognized that it was not only okay to be a strong woman who loved Jesus, I honored Him when I walked in my strengths and the way He made me. I shifted from hating the Proverbs 31 woman because I knew I could never be her (nor did I want to) to realizing that she was the original wild woman—someone I could aspire to follow.

I know I am not the only woman who has felt trapped because she was taught a caricature of the Proverbs 31 woman. As a result, we get the idea that we somehow manage to not be enough but also be too much at the same time. We are never able to keep up with the ever-growing list of demands of what we should do and who we should be, while simultaneously feeling judged for being too loud, too opinionated, too emotional.

Personally, I like to think that the Proverbs 31 woman lived with the same tension but was never ruled by it. I think she was fully aware of what needed to be done and what was required of her, but she never let her to-do list dictate her worth. I believe she was loud and opinionated and sometimes emotional, but instead of letting that make her feel like too much, she recognized that these traits were what made her human.

In short, I've come to love rather than loathe the Proverbs 31 woman. I no longer see her as coming from a mold I never wanted to fit but as a guide I'm honored to follow. And I never want to see her weaponized against women to further the not-enough-but-too-much narrative. After carefully studying this passage, I'm taking back the Proverbs 31 woman so I see her in the way the Father intended her to be seen—as a strong leader who knew exactly who she was and whose she was.

When I began digging, I was fascinated to read verse 1 and discover that the words of Proverbs 31:10-31 were attributed to a woman who was advising her son, King Lemuel, about the kind of wife he should look for. For so long we've been taught that these verses were written from a man's perspective to tell women what they should be, but in fact it is primarily a list of what men should look for in the women they will marry. Today we also look at it as a punch list for us girls, but that was not how it was originally read. Doesn't knowing the passage was intended for a man change our entire perspective?

Interestingly, do you know what the Hebrew phrase for "a virtuous wife" (verse 10, NKJV) in those first few words of this section is? *Eshet khayil.* *Eshet* can be translated as "woman" or "wife," but Scripture also applies the term *khayil* to men. For instance, that word shows up in the term "mighty men of valor" found in 2 Kings 24:14. Interestingly, Ruth, the Moabite widow, was also called *khayil* by the Israelites and by Boaz, her eventual husband, because of the courage and loyalty she showed when she followed her mother-in-law back to Bethlehem. (The complete story is told in the book of Ruth.)

So in Proverbs 31, Lemuel's mom tells him to search out a woman who is a champion. A woman of hard-won victory and reward. A woman of strength. This makes me simultaneously scrunch my eyes in frustration and puff my chest in pride. Can you imagine if the people who taught us about Proverbs 31 had told us she was actually a tenacious and spirited woman? One who wouldn't take no for an answer? A woman of valor, not timidity. Mighty not feeble. It would have changed the game.

And that's what we learn from just the first three words. What about her relationship with her husband? Yep, that's solid too. So solid he completely trusts her. He is so confident in her abilities and trustworthiness that he knows his deepest, darkest secrets are safe with her. She makes his life so much better in every way that she is considered a gain, not a burden. Even before I knew I wanted to be a wife, I knew this was the kind of partner I wanted to be—able to stand on my own two feet, confident and secure in who God made me so I wouldn't constantly lean on my boo to tell me who I am. But so often Christianity redefines those traits as being "too much."

Listen up: Knowing who you are in Christ is not prideful. Walking in the gifts He's given you is not arrogance. And *man* have we gotten this all upside down and twisted. We've been taught so much about humility we have no idea what godly confidence looks like. That's not to say there wasn't and still isn't so much room for growth, sanctification, and sanding off the rough edges. I always want to look, sound, and live more like Jesus.

When I moved beyond the one-dimensional woman I was introduced to at church, I was thrilled to discover that the Proverbs 31 woman and I share an entrepreneurial spirit. Verses 13-16 unveil a busy, hardworking, and creative woman who is legit investing and making a profit! That doesn't sound like a woman who lives under the thumb of her husband, who is insecure and doesn't know what she's doing. I personally have never bought a vineyard, but that sounds like a whole situation. A few books later the prophet Isaiah details what's involved in the management of a vineyard: "He dug it up and cleared it of stones and planted it with the choicest vines. He built a watchtower in it and cut out a winepress as well" (Isaiah 5:2, NIV). That's a lot of work!

Proverbs 31:16 (NKJV) tells us she "considers" a field, meaning she is thoughtful and wise and in the end moves forward with her purchase. Maybe this woman doesn't know what she is doing right away and has to learn. Maybe she has lengthy conversations with her husband about the vineyard she's found and her dreams of producing wine. Not every woman is born to be a businesswoman, but most women I know desire to have something that is theirs, something they create and produce and are proud to put their name on. The Proverbs 31 woman is no different.

MY OWN KIND OF WOMAN

One reason I often felt like I was "too much" growing up in Christian culture was my strength. Not necessarily physically—I'm not going to win any strongman competitions anytime soon. But I'm made of tough stuff. I'm resilient nearly to a fault, and my bounce-back rate sometimes gives my husband whiplash. He can't believe how quickly I can get over things. My whole life I have looked up to women who buck the system and do things their own way. The virtuous wife is noted for her strength (see Proverbs 31:17-18, 20, NKJV): strength in action, physical strength (she "strengthens her arms"), mental strength ("she perceives that her merchandise is good"), and moral strength ("she extends her hand to the poor").

I was lucky to have grown up on the classics. While kids my age were watching *The Little Mermaid*, I was fostering a growing affinity for Katharine Hepburn in films like *The African Queen*. Her portrayal of Jo March in *Little Women* kind of changed my life, as I'm sure Saoirse Ronan's depiction of Jo does for strong-willed little girls today. As I watched the 1933 film when I was young, I noticed that Hepburn looked different from the women around her, which drew me in literally and figuratively. I actually scooted closer to the screen, hoping I could suck in some of her unapologetic "me"-ness.

We can't know whether the Proverbs 31 woman bucked the system of her day, but the more that I learn about her, the more I think she probably did. I've come to think maybe she was a little more Jo March than Pollyanna. And now when I stand up against injustice or use my voice in situations that require me to be strong, I don't feel shame—I feel like the kind of woman King Lemuel's mom wanted him to marry. I love her for her entrepreneurial spirit, the way she fearlessly provided for her family and made investments that would serve her interests. Sometimes the tendrils of guilt try to climb up my neck, whispering that I shouldn't work hard or make money to provide, but the truth of the Proverbs 31 woman pushes them back. "She sets about her work vigorously; her arms are strong for her tasks. She sees that her trading is profitable, and her lamp does not go out at night" (verses 17-18, NIV).

After years of believing that the perfect Christian woman did nothing but read her Bible, tend to the children, and say yes to

> WE DON'T NEED TO TRY BEING WHAT SOMEONE ELSE TOLD US IS RIGHT AND CHRISTLIKE; WE JUST NEED TO WALK IN THE FULLNESS OF THE GOODNESS OF GOD AND BE AN EXPRESSION OF THAT.

every request, I feel safe now in the truth that women of God read their Bibles and tend to the children (if that's God's plan) but also say yes to what God asks of them and have no problem working, creating, and contributing. I think that's my favorite part of my Proverbs 31 deep dive—the subsequent freedom to be who God made me to be, a woman with a spirit of power, love, and self-control, not fear (see 2 Timothy 1:7).

We were meant to live without asking for others' approval. Without fear of what they'll think. In full awareness of our humanity and need for a Savior, we can walk through our days knowing the God who created the aurora borealis also took the time to make us. He made us champions, victorious, strong; maybe a little less Doris Day and a little more Katharine Hepburn. And He loves our tenacity. We don't need to try being what someone else told us is right and Christlike; we just need to walk in the fullness of the goodness of God and be an expression of that.

Maybe you, too, need to emancipate your version of the Proverbs 31 woman. Maybe the church has told you you're supposed to be someone you're not and you've spent your life trying to fit that mold. Be free, sister. Be who He made you without question or apology. Work hard for His glory and rest in His goodness.

I think that's who the Proverbs 31 woman was. That's the kind of woman King Lemuel's mama wanted him to end up with—someone secure in her Creator and nothing else.

Chapter 7

WHAT'S IN IT
(THE BIBLE) FOR ME?

There are known knowns. There are things we know we know.
We also know there are known unknowns. That is to say, we know there's
some things we do not know. But there are also unknown unknowns,
the ones we don't know we don't know.

DONALD RUMSFELD

I LOVE RUMSFELD'S QUOTE. I know it's a bit of a tongue twister—a little Seussian as well—but that's probably why I love it. Here's one thing I know I don't know: how to parallel park. Much to the chagrin of both my father and husband, I simply cannot do it. I will straight up circle a block until I find a place to pull in, no matter how many parallel spots they may silently point out as we drive by. I don't know how to parallel park because I've never tried to learn. I have decided I don't want to know how to parallel park because it freaks me out and I'm convinced I'll never be any good at it. Maybe by the time this book is in your hands I'll have gotten over my irrational refusal and will be able to whip into any parallel spot in five seconds flat. We'll see. But for now I don't know how to parallel park because I've never taken the time to learn.

There are a lot of other things I don't know. I don't know how to complete the formula for general relativity or how to make a risotto or fold a fitted sheet. But I'll tell you what I do know: I know my Bible. No, I can't spit it out verbatim. And honestly, I'm pretty terrible at remembering the references that go along with the verses I've memorized. But I know what the Bible says and I know what it doesn't say.

That wasn't always the case.

I spent a lot of my life as a believer having a general knowledge of Scripture. I went through seasons where all my Bible did was gather dust on my nightstand or I didn't even know where it was. And there were other times when I diligently opened it every single morning. I knew well-known verses like Jeremiah 29:11 and could usually flip to the book I was looking for in a few tries, thanks to those Bible drills at my private Christian elementary school. I knew that Scripture was God-breathed and that Paul wrote a ton of the New Testament. I could find the verses I needed to apply to my life with the help of a quick Google search. I was familiar with it the way I'm familiar with driving a car, but I lacked the finesse and knowledge required to parallel park it.

I spent most of my time reading the comfy New Testament books because, to be honest, the rest of it stressed me out. Why is everyone's name approximately seventeen syllables long? Have you ever read Genesis 10? It's basically just lists of names! Or what about Revelation? I feel like you need one of those decoder rings out of a cereal box to make any sense of that one.

I wasn't willing to touch a lot of Scripture because I didn't understand it and therefore it just didn't really matter to me. I read the Bible like a textbook, skimming some parts, rereading others, and underlining what jumped out at me as important. I never really used any tools alongside it, I didn't study it any deeper than what was on the page in front of me, and I absolutely cherry-picked whatever I wanted out of it.

Context and depth, memorization and study are all concepts I implemented in various other areas of study (ask me anything about American history or *Seinfeld*), but for some reason it had never occurred to me that Scripture was something to be studied. It was a book—a very important, holy, special one—but still a book. I assumed it was meant only to be read, not studied, by someone like me. So like many other Christians, I read it when I thought about it, or when I needed it, or when someone else reminded me to. I understood it on a surface level and, therefore, was only able to apply it to my life that way. But I didn't *know* it. And because I didn't know it, I didn't know God as well as I could have.

It's not that if we don't know our Bible we don't know God. There are still thousands of people groups who don't yet have the Bible translated into their native tongue but who still know something about Him. However, there are many things about God, and therefore about us, that we can't know if we don't know His Word. We have a more shallow understanding of who God is, who He has always been, and who He will always be.

And if I don't understand who God is then I can't know who He says I am. When I think back to the years I loved God but not His Word, I realize I was like someone who holds the keys to a really powerful car but doesn't know how to put them in the ignition. I knew God and absolutely experienced Him and loved Him, but I had very little understanding of who He is. Having grown up in a Christian home, I had the basic biblical knowledge needed to know the foundational principles, but it wasn't until my relationship with Christ became my own in my college years that I became aware of how much I didn't know about Him. It was then that spending time in Scripture became an important part of my walk and not a throwaway, optional element. Once I understood that I had access to pages upon pages of intimate conversations with the Father I loved so much, I felt a little ridiculous that I hadn't been digging into it already.

Because I had never studied Exodus, I couldn't fully understand that God is the God of generations. That He is a Father who works through His children and their families. By digging deep into the history and stories woven through Exodus, I grew to love the God of Abraham, Isaac, and Jacob (see Exodus 3:6). When I understood the God whom Moses knew (the same God we know), I began to grasp the importance of lineage as well as God's unchangeable, immutable characteristics. This impacted the way I looked at parenting almost immediately. I had been operating from an in-the-trenches, covered-in-spit-up mindset after having two girls two years apart. Imparting God's goodness and character to my children became much higher on my list of priorities, shaping how I did everything from reading the Bible to them to cutting the crusts off their PB&Js. It sounds cliché, and I am not a Pinterest-perfect mother by any stretch of the imagination, but I can tell you that understanding a new-to-me facet of God infused my motherhood with meaning. The days felt less mundane, less repetitive, and more intentional. The little things grew in importance as the idea of legacy grew in my mind. Of all the important things I may do on this planet, leaving behind a genealogy of faithful children who love Jesus became most important, and motherhood became less an obligation and more of a gift.

I've come to appreciate the value of applying Scripture, knowing it is meant to light our path (see Psalm 119:105). It's really hard to light a candle, though, if you don't know how fire works. And the more I dug into the Word—really dug in—using it instead of only devotionals as my primary connection to God, that illumination spread.

Like the first time I studied Revelation. *Oof.* Anyone who's dipped a toe in those waters knows it's not only intense, but freaking confusing. Who is the woman (see Revelation 12)? Why does the beast in chapter 13 seem like he'd be better fit for a Frankenstein remake? Why are there so many booming voices? But for me specifically, beginning to understand the dichotomy between the Lion and the Lamb in chapter 5 profoundly impacted how I see and understand Jesus:

> I saw a mighty angel proclaiming in a loud voice, "Who is worthy to break the seals and open the scroll?" But no one in heaven or on earth or under the earth could open the scroll or even look inside it. I wept and wept because no one was found who was worthy to open the scroll or look inside. Then one of the elders said to me, "Do not weep! See, the Lion of the tribe of Judah, the Root of David, has triumphed. He is able to open the scroll and its seven seals."
>
> Then I saw a Lamb, looking as if it had been slain, standing at the center of the throne, encircled by the four living creatures and the elders. . . . He went and took the scroll from the right hand of him who sat on the throne. And when he had taken it, the four living creatures and the twenty-four elders fell down before the Lamb.
>
> REVELATION 5:2-8, NIV

I'm a fighter by nature. There's a good chance I was in more fistfights than you before my Jesus-loving days. I'm just naturally combative and always up for a debate. I've even been known to perceive that someone is itching for a fight when they're not. So Jesus the conqueror makes sense to me. Jesus the Lion, I can get behind. But the Lamb? Hard pass. I'm no lamb, I'm no sacrifice, I'm no lie-down-in-green-pastures type. But should I be?

When we think power, we think king of the jungle, but this representative of the Kingdom of Heaven is shown as the Lamb, symbolizing humility, gentleness, and sacrifice. Once I understood Jesus as both Lion and Lamb, I was better equipped to walk through life striving to be both as well. To conquer and defend as well as to submit and choose gentleness when the situation requires it. If I didn't know my Bible, it would be quite easy for someone to teach me that Christ was one or the other and for me to believe that I couldn't possibly be an amalgamation of both.

HONEST TO GOD

The Bible character I resonate with most is David. Our stories are similar—outside of my complete inexperience with sheep or nine-foot-tall Philistine soldiers—but strip it down and they're definitely similar. Humble beginnings, a quick ascent to the spotlight, struggles with some sexual sin, a healthy dose of depression, lots of questions and friendship issues. Yeah. I feel David. But aside from sensing that I'd discovered a kindred spirit in him, I found his experiences with God foreign yet intriguing when I studied his life. He's definitely not the first nor the last Bible character to do this, but I was shocked by how he laid it out with God in a no-holds-barred way, flinging questions and concerns and what even seemed like accusations occasionally.

Like in Psalm 22:1-2, when homeboy gets dramatic with God, asking, "My God, my God, why have you forsaken me? Why are you so far from saving me, so far from my cries of anguish? My

God, I cry out by day, but you do not answer, by night, but I find no rest" (NIV). Like . . . can David do that? Obviously, he could. God welcomed the stripped-down, rock-bottom David into His presence just as much as the stately, pulled-together version of him. Even better, God Himself never changed. No matter how up in his feelings David got, no matter how distressed or distant he was, no matter how far David strayed from God (even when he had his baby mama's husband killed—okay, we don't have that in common either), the Lord never changed. And when I understood that about David's God, I knew it was true about mine as well.

When you don't let the Bible tell you who God is and therefore who you are, someone or something else will. Maybe it'll be the internet. Maybe it will be your relationships or the obnoxious critic that lives in your head rent-free. If you're not saturated in the Word, you won't have anything to hold that representation up against and say whether it's true or not. The opinions and judgments telling you who or what you should be are going to enter your orbit; that's inevitable in the unbelievably loud world we live in today. But just because something enters your atmosphere doesn't mean you have to let it stay there, take root, and become real. Just because a thought flits through your mind doesn't mean it should take hold. That's another thing Scripture has taught me.

The weapons we fight with are not the weapons of
the world. On the contrary, they have divine power
to demolish strongholds. We demolish arguments and
every pretension that sets itself up against the knowledge
of God, and we take captive every thought to make it
obedient to Christ.

2 CORINTHIANS 10:4-5, NIV

The weapons Paul mentions? They are the armor of God listed in Ephesians 6. And what is one of those pieces of armor—"the sword of the Spirit, which is the word of God" (verse 17, NLT)? The other protective parts—including our faith, salvation, and truth (see verses 14, 16-17)—are all found, understood, and cultivated by being in the Word. Being steeped in Scripture is the most effective way to take your thoughts captive. The Bible becomes the filter through which you separate lies and truth. Understanding who you are and whose you are from a biblical standpoint makes it incredibly difficult for the enemy to convince you otherwise.

Every day I watch women let the world—whether secular or even church spaces—tell them who they are. If that describes you, you are probably suffering from a severe case of identity whiplash because our culture cannot make up its mind about who we should be. One minute you're supposed to be a tough boss babe building your empire with a baby on your hip while working out eight days a week; the next you need to be a homeschooling, make-your-own-yogurt naturopath who teaches your children to thread a loom after meditation. The mold never stops morphing, the bar never stops moving, and at the end of every day you're left to ask if you did enough, if you were enough, or if maybe you were too much. Unfortunately, the American church doesn't land this plane much more smoothly than the world does.

Are you meant to be a servant-hearted, quiet Sunday school volunteer? Will you ever be allowed to study anything other than the stereotypical Proverbs 31 woman (see chapter 6)? There's nothing wrong with either of those women, but if you don't naturally fit that pattern, church can be rough. If you're inherently a loud-mouthed leader with a rebel streak, a lot of churches don't know what to do with you. But you know who does? The One who made you that way. And you know where there are lots of stories of women like you? Scripture. It was like a balm to my mouthy soul when I began to dig into the Old Testament and met women like Miriam (see Exodus 2:1-10; Exodus 15:20; Numbers 12), Deborah (see Judges 4–5), Huldah (see 2 Kings 22:14-20; 2 Chronicles 34:22-28), and Jael (see Judges 4) who changed the course of history by being exactly who God had created them to be. If you are allowing anyone other than God to define your identity, you are missing a huge part of the puzzle. Even if you're finding out who you are from good places like relationships or community, church or motherhood, the only place you'll discover the full, beautiful, complex picture is in the Word of God. That is why I fully believe that if more of us would turn away from Instagram and toward our Bibles, we would be a generation of women confident in our identities in Christ, dangerous to the enemies of the Kingdom of God.

> IF MORE OF US WOULD TURN AWAY FROM INSTAGRAM AND TOWARD OUR BIBLES, WE WOULD BE A GENERATION OF WOMEN CONFIDENT IN OUR IDENTITIES IN CHRIST, DANGEROUS TO THE ENEMIES OF THE KINGDOM OF GOD.

JUST READ IT

So we know reading our Bibles is important, but why don't we do it? I refuse to believe it's laziness or even our superbusy lives, because if we have time to scroll we have time to crack open the Word. No, I believe we often don't read our Bibles for two reasons: We either think other people's imparting of the Word is enough for us or we're too overwhelmed to get started. I've lived in both camps, so I want to tell you what actually happens in these spaces.

We value and rely on other people's commentary. I'm going to be blunt here because I love you: Instagram is not your Bible.

Devotionals are not your Bible. This book is not your Bible. Influencers aren't your Jesus, and authors are never going to be your Savior. Stop looking to them to tell you the story only God can tell. Stop treating the internet as a substitute for the infallible Word of Christ and the goodness of God you'll find there. Other people's analysis will never be enough. This doesn't mean you cannot or should not learn from others in online spaces or that you shouldn't be sharing what God is teaching you there. But it will never be a replacement because we are humans and we can't help but add our humanity to everything we touch.

This corruption isn't always malicious like high schoolers who spread rumors that morph with every person; sometimes it happens simply because we're imperfect humans attempting to tell a perfect story. We add our own spin out of our desire to understand, or we allow our baggage and life experiences to taint the stories. I think this can happen even when learning from pastors and Bible teachers, not only on the internet. Because of our reverence and respect for the pulpit, we sometimes abandon the art of critical thinking. It is okay to question what someone is teaching you if it doesn't line up with Scripture. But you can't even do that if you don't know Scripture yourself. If the only dose of Bible learning you're getting is coming from someone else, how will you ever know they've led you astray until you're off the path? There are many great reasons to know your Bible for yourself, but being sure you're sticking to the truth of it is a big one.

We're too overwhelmed to start. The Bible is a big book. And it contains names like Maher-shalal-hash-baz (I'm not making that up—see Isaiah 8:3) and stories of she-bears tearing people apart for making fun of a prophet, not to mention an uncomfortable amount of incest. It's 1,189 chapters long and takes the most

WHAT'S IN IT (THE BIBLE) FOR ME?

aggressive readers at least a year to finish the whole thing. All in all, the Bible intimidates a lot of people, so they never start reading it.

If you fall into this camp, can I give you a little bit of encouragement? Just start. You don't have to undertake some grand theological study; you don't need to take pages of notes or own the right kind of highlighter. Start in the Gospels and immerse yourself in the life of Jesus. Meet the God-man who gave His life for yours, and study His life, from His birth to His death, and the movement that He began. Encounter the disciples in all of their humanity, chosen by Jesus to walk alongside Him through life. Then move over to Romans and learn from Paul about salvation, God's sovereignty and righteousness, judgment, and spiritual growth. When you're feeling a little more confident, start dipping into the Old Testament and hit up Psalms or Proverbs. Your process doesn't have to be perfect; you don't have to spend hours at a time on it, and here's your permission slip to skip over the big words that overwhelm you.

FIND A GUIDE

Here is another great tip someone gave me when I began my own pursuit of biblical knowledge: Find someone you know who does this well and ask them to teach you. In every other area of study, we learn from professors, teachers, mentors, and guides; why wouldn't we do that for the most important book we'll ever read? Your guide doesn't necessarily have to be a theologian in title. It could be a woman from your local community who has a deep and beautiful understanding of Scripture. Put aside the awkwardness and tell her you would like to learn from her, if she's willing. I imagine it would be a great gift to her as well. To avoid falling into the trap of letting someone else tell you what to think about the Bible, be an active participant when you meet: ask questions, take notes, and do some of your own research.

However you get started, I encourage you to intentionally spend time in the Word every day for a month. I'd bet my non-existent farm that by the end of those thirty days, you'll have a better understanding of God, what He's done for you, and what He has to say about you. I suspect those thirty days won't be enough, and you'll find your stride. You can start picking up commentaries or concordances, expand your library and your understanding, and just fall in love with the Word of God. But you have to start. Because if you don't, your Bible will continue to be an unknown known, and your life will be lesser for it.

Chapter 8

WOULD JESUS BE A JERK?

Handle them carefully, for words
have more power than atom bombs.

PEARL STRACHAN HURD

I KNOW THIS IS GOING TO COME AS A SHOCK to those of you who know me (and for those who don't, trust me, it's true), but there is a specific subset of people on the internet who very much do not like me. They consider my theology too heavy on grace, too focused on God's loving-kindness and not enough on the Ten Commandments. They are highly offended by my belief that the ultimate goal of the Christian life is not to stop sinning, but to embody Christlike love. And I'll be honest, your girl is usually up for a good internet battle, especially when it comes down to law versus grace. So round and round we've gone for years, locking horns over topics like Mosaic law and utter depravity until we get bored with each other and move on, only to come back to it down the road. As time has passed and these conversations have contin-ued, I've come to realize my issue is far less with their theology (even though we do fundamentally disagree on a lot of things) and much more with their *delivery*.

Let's get the elephant in the room out of the way up front: I have been known to let a snide comment fly a time or two myself. I've been told I need to control my facial expressions and adjust my delivery plenty of times. Like the day we attended the funeral for my husband's sweet grandfather and I had a front row seat to one of the most theologically unsound sermons I've ever heard. I eventually received a sharp elbow to the ribs from my husband, who whispered, "You need to change your face." Apparently, my distaste was written all over my scrunched eyebrows and down-turned mouth without my even realizing it.

There are plenty of stories of Jeremy uttering a soft but mildly embarrassed "Babe" under his breath when I say brazenly inappropriate things in social settings (even though everyone was for sure thinking it). I am naturally snarky and sarcastic and maybe a little bit witty and incapable of hiding how I feel about things. Sure, there's a time and a place for a well-placed smart-aleck comment among people with whom you've earned the right to be blunt.

But I have learned that the way you speak to people, especially about sensitive topics, matters deeply. For instance, I've found that snark really isn't necessary and is, in fact, extraordinarily off-putting, when talking about the Word of God. I feel a natural reverence both when I'm speaking about Scripture and when speaking to others in an attempt to help them understand it. Because of that, I've worked overtime to curtail my often-natural sarcasm in these conversations. Do I do this perfectly? No. Do I still sometimes get spicy with people online? Absolutely. But when it comes down to talking about matters of our Father, I do my best to leave the banter at the door.

Those I like to call Instagram Pharisees take a different approach. Maybe you're lucky and haven't encountered these individuals, but if you have, you know exactly what I'm talking about. They know more about Scripture than you do, and they're here to remind you of all the ways you're depraved, unworthy, and sinful. Everything is problematic; there's something amiss in everything from worship music to personality tests, and they're going to tell you about it. At the end of the day, you know these people for what they stand against and what they don't like instead of what and whom they love.

Unfortunately, these people do not exist exclusively on Instagram. They're in our churches and in our neighborhoods. When they're not hiding behind a keyboard, some of them will say the most atrocious things straight to your face. In the end, it can just feel like they've missed it. Like somewhere during their Bible reading journey, they missed the good stuff about grace and gentleness, loving-kindness and mercy. Now I won't pretend to know their motives. If I trust the Holy Spirit in the people I like, I have to trust He is in those I find less than likable. But what I do feel is fair to talk about is the way they communicate their message.

As someone fluent in sarcasm, I understand how easy it is to fall into this biblical banter trap. In the early days of our marriage my husband once asked if we could come up with code words to use when I was being sarcastic and when I was serious because, to be quite honest, he couldn't always tell which I was and it was confusing for him. So I get it. When you're passionate about something as important as the Word of God, it can be frustrating to hear people twist its contents to mean something it doesn't. I understand that fiery need to not only teach others Scripture but also to defend it!

Scripture is clear about being wary of false teachers and those who aim to twist and contort the Bible and lead people astray. Paul spends a *ton* of time in his letters to Timothy instructing his young assistant to be careful so that bogus theology doesn't rise up in the church of Ephesus,[1] especially those beliefs that are more publicly acceptable than the gospel truth. Over the last few years we've seen a steady rise in the number of Bible teachers bending to the pressure and abandoning what the Bible teaches for what is more acceptable by the public's standards. It's heartbreaking and it's dangerous, to say the least. So, yes, we absolutely need to be able to test the spirits to know whether they're from God (see 1 John 4:1) and not allow ourselves to be tossed to and fro by different doctrines (see Ephesians 4:14). We also need to study our Bibles so we can better know God and His Word, which enables us to walk in righteousness.

In 1 Peter 3, the apostle Peter instructs believers to "always [be] prepared to make a defense to anyone who asks you for a reason for the hope that is in you . . ." (1 Peter 3:15, ESV). There is a pandemic of biblical illiteracy, especially in American Christianity, and therefore many of us are unable to explain why and what we believe, as well as why we hold hope in who we hold our hope in. But there is another movement sweeping through Christianity that is equally problematic, and it starts with those who disregard the last six words of 1 Peter 3:15: "yet do it with gentleness and respect."

If you can't tell me why you believe what you believe while being gentle and respectful, there is a high chance I'm not going to want to hear anything you have to say. And this is the disconnect with the Instagram Pharisee movement. Honestly, they're right about a lot of things (do we ever 100 percent agree with someone, especially about theology?). I often find myself agreeing with what they say, just not how they say it. Still, something within me pushes away from these individuals. I walk away after listening to them feeling less than, beaten over the head, or unsure about what I know (and not in a good way). I encourage you to listen to those nudges from the Holy Spirit because here's what I've come to know about my Jesus: He doesn't deal in guilt and doesn't speak to us in sarcastic terms.

I've grown wary of these voices (especially in the Instagram space) who have taken it upon themselves to build their entire ministry around the cause of calling out false teachers. Entire Instagram accounts exclusively post content like "false teacher Fridays," tearing down Bible teachers. And sure, many of them practice questionable theology. But can you imagine if Jesus' entire earthly ministry was devoted to this same cause? How empty would His teachings be? What would have drawn people to His love?

Jesus was direct and to the point, especially with those who attempted to bind others in the needless bondage of law. He and His apostles did on occasion call out false teachers and prophets. But His habitual lifestyle was one of grace, love, and truth. It dripped off every word He spoke, even when those words were hard to digest. Every single thing Jesus did was drenched in the love that He would eventually exemplify on the cross, and we should try to do the same. So I'm not disputing that "keeping watch" is an important facet of the Christian life or that there are tough theological conversations to be had, but I have a question:

What's the point of it all?

SIN SICK

For a long time I believed the entire mission of the Christian life was to stop sinning and to help other people keep from sinning. I thought every one of my waking moments was to be devoted solely to the all-important task of escaping sin so I could become more like Jesus. I spent a lot of time stuck in guilt and shame, beating myself up for getting it wrong or letting a choice word fly.

I swear that every time I went to the gym, I spent the entire walk back to my car apologizing to God for noticing the butt of the guy working out next to me. I'd promise not to do it again, beating myself up mentally because surely the Proverbs 31 woman never noticed any guy's rear end. Most of my time with the Lord was spent repenting and apologizing, asking Him to help me do it better tomorrow. I was hyperfocused on my depravity, inability, and dirtiness, and it was an exhausting and difficult way to live. Not only was I tired, but I looked at God as my disciplinarian instead of my Father. He wasn't my friend; He was the one who pointed out all the ways I got it wrong, all the sin that consumed me, and was frankly embarrassed that we were talking yet again about butts. I spent a long time under the rule of shame, and for years I missed out on the opportunity to walk in the freedom that the Cross afforded me. When I look back, I can see that part of the problem was the teachers I was learning from.

Instead of pointing me to the finished work of the Cross and the truth that God's divine power had given me everything required for life and godliness (see 2 Peter 1:3), these teachers focused on sin—the power of sin, the danger of sin, as well as our utter depravity and fleshly desires. I'm grateful that I began studying under pastors and teachers who helped me understand that living that way, hyperfocused on sin and regret, was not living in the freedom that Christ gave us through the Cross. Often when I talk about this, people assume I'm saying sin is unimportant or that ceasing to sin isn't a part of the Christian life, which is absolutely not the case. Sin is awful. Sin was bad enough that Jesus needed to die to defeat it and free us from its power. It's not that avoiding sin isn't a critical element of the life of a believer, it's just that I believe there's more to our Christian walk than that.

> I give you a new command: Love one another. Just as I
> have loved you, you are also to love one another. By this
> everyone will know that you are my disciples, if you love
> one another.
>
> JOHN 13:34-35

In other words, stopping sinning is not the ultimate goal of the Christian life here on earth. Love is.

I like to put myself in the place of the disciples as they listen to Jesus share this message at the Last Supper. Jesus has just predicted that one of them would betray Him. In fact, he has essentially called out Judas as the one who would do it and told him to go ahead and get after it. Once Judas leaves, Jesus leans in to His closest people and tells them this: *Love each other. Love each other like I've loved you during our time together. Let people know exactly who you are and whose you are by how well you love one another.*

This is freaking radical to His disciples. Remember they are still living under the heavy burden of the Mosaic law—social laws, moral laws, laws about food and feasts and sacrifices and offerings. The list of laws is so long it is humanly impossible to keep up with them. And in this moment, Jesus turns it all on its head and gives them a new greatest commandment—love. He doesn't tell them to make sure they don't sin. He doesn't say to be sure their brother doesn't sin. Nor does He ask them to be sure everyone knows who the false teachers are. He leaves them with the instruction to love.

Profound and exponential love is the whole point of the Christian walk. It's meant to influence and touch every aspect of our lives, and everything we do should pour out from a place of loving people because Christ loved us first. Out of this love we will walk in righteousness and our desire to sin will die along with the hold our flesh has on us.

Admittedly, we've gotten the definition of love a little wonky, even within the church. We've come to believe that if you love someone, you'll accept and encourage all of their life choices and cheer them on, regardless if what they're doing goes against who they really are in Christ. But verse 6 of the most popular description of what love is—1 Corinthians 13—tells us love can't rejoice in wrongdoing.

So sometimes love looks like telling friends who are making bad choices that God created them for more than the way they're choosing to live. And sometimes love looks like pointing out problematic elements of a teacher's theology. Love isn't always rainbows and rose petals and agreeing with everything that comes out of a person's mouth. Love is tough. Love bears wrongdoing and turns the other cheek. Love doesn't need to be right all the time, but at the end of the day, it pursues truth. I bear the burden of telling the hard truths right alongside you. It is a monumental commission to hold the truth of God in your hands, knowing that you need to share it with the world.

But how you do it matters.

HOW DO WE LOVE LOVINGLY?

I've come to learn that love without truth is enabling, and the truth without love is usually just . . . rude. I really do believe that by and large, the Instagram Pharisees have good intentions. Look, I've been there—just wanting people to know the truth of the Bible and passionately not wanting others to be led astray by attractive messages that don't line up with the Word. And there really is a time and a place for speaking up. But we have to quit being so dang snarky about it. How are we going to draw nonbelievers into the family of God if all they encounter when they run into us is a bunch of cynicism and the feeling that everyone is looking down their noses at them? I worry that we've lost touch with the Jesus who lived here on earth. He dined and associated with the least desirables of society. He touched infected lepers (which was a major no-no). This is the man who refused to condemn the woman caught in adultery and instead told her "go and sin no more" (John 8:11, NLT). He's the man who met the woman at the well and saw straight through her bull and offered her eternal life.

Jesus radically changed the trajectory of people's lives and decisions by loving them first. He always led with love, even in the toughest of situations. Even when people were dead wrong. Even when they drove nails through His wrists to pin Him to a cross He did not deserve, He led with love. The primary command He left us with calls us to do the same.

But you cannot love what you mock.

Think of something you love. Like, really love. Maybe it's a hobby or a place, a subject, even a TV show. For example, I really love history. Specifically, American history, but I can sit for hours on end reading dusty old books about time periods that date back to Caesar, even if the type is so small it hurts my eyes. I own an oversized notepad exclusively for the purpose of mapping out historical events and constitutional amendments. On a romantic trip to Las Vegas one year, I dragged my husband off the glitzy strip to visit every museum we could hit. (I give a 10 out of 10 to The Mob Museum and encourage you to visit if you're ever in the neighborhood.) My history nerd card is nice and crisp, and I keep it laminated in my pocket protector. I love this subject so deeply that I cannot fathom making fun of the study and subject of history.

Conversely, I cannot speak about history in condescending terms to someone who does not know or love history because I so deeply want them to know and love the wonder of times gone by. I can't risk pushing them away with my tone. When conversations about history rev up and I notice a participant who is uninterested (or even ill-informed), my response cannot be "Well, you're wrong and you're an idiot" because all that will do is make them even more convinced that history is not worth knowing.

> JESUS CALLED US TO LOVE OTHERS. AND HIS WORD IS A TOOL TO HELP US DO THAT BETTER, NOT A WEAPON WITH WHICH TO CUT DOWN OUR SISTERS.

Shouldn't this be all the more true about the Word of God? We're surrounded by flesh and blood souls in crisis who are at risk of missing eternity with the Father, and we're out here kind of being jerks about it? Shouldn't our words be like honey—"sweet to the soul and healthy for the body" (Proverbs 16:24, NLT)? I really do believe we cannot mock what we love or love what we mock. This is my sticking point with Instagram Pharisees. They have passion and knowledge, but they lack love. Ultimately, Jesus called us to love others. And His Word is a tool to help us do that better, not a weapon with which to cut down our sisters. Yes, the Bible is the sword of the Spirit, but it is meant to be used in the battle against powers and principalities because that is where our real battle wages, not among one another. And this is where I think we can get it wrong. Though we're in the midst of a war, we're so wrapped up in debunking and disputing other people that we're spending our time poking at a problematic hole in the ground. Distraction is one of the enemy's best tools to render us ineffective. When we are primarily focused on stopping sin, exposing false teachers, and beating people over the head with doctrine, we forget that love is our greatest weapon in the war for souls.

So tell the truth. Pull what grows in the dark into the light. Expose strongholds and false doctrine. Rescue your sister from the pits of sin and false belief systems. But do it because you love her too much to leave her there. Let love lead and know that it will likely guide you into difficult conversations and hard topics, but trust that it will never leave you there to do the work alone. Throw aside the false confidence gained by speaking out of sarcasm and condescension. Instead, get down to eye level with your sister whom you love so much and give her the gospel. Because she needs this good news, and she needs it the way only you can share it with her.

Chapter 9

WHY DOES IT TAKE SO LONG TO HEAL?

Trauma creates changes you don't choose.
Healing is about creating change you do choose.
MICHELE ROSENTHAL

TRAUMA HAS A WAY OF CHANGING US on the most molecular level. Ask anyone who has walked through harrowing times, and they'll likely tell you it changed them, whether they wanted it to or not. When my older daughter, Pacey Claire (who, yes, is absolutely named for Pacey Witter of *Dawson's Creek*), was just over a year old, she experienced a thirty-five-minute-long febrile seizure, which can occur when a small child's body is fighting off a virus accompanied by a high fever. The seizures are usually about five minutes in length, and while scary, they are innocuous. They can present as full-blown grand mal seizures or simply the child going limp for a few seconds. But for thirty-five minutes, my tiny first-born child's body shook and seized, her eyes rolled back in her head, and she grunted and gasped for breath.

When the seizure began, we had just changed Pacey into paja-mas, and she was lying slack on top of me on the couch. Her body jumped once, and my mom intuition somehow knew what was happening, even though it never had before. I handed her limp, seizing body to my husband, Jeremy, and immediately jumped on Google to see what we needed to do—finding that if the seizure lasted longer than five minutes, we were to call an ambulance. The five minutes quickly passed, and as I punched in 911, hysteria began to kick in. I wish I could tell you I was calm in the face of terror, but as I explained the situation to the operator, I morphed into the mother you hear on recordings of 911 calls—hysterical, inconsolable, straight up just freaking out. The operator instructed us to lay her on the ground, strip her down to her diaper, and ensure she didn't choke on her tongue—things no parent should ever have to do.

We were blessed to live right around the corner from a fire station, and the paramedics arrived at our home minutes after I called. They loaded her into the ambulance, and I rode alongside my seizing child to the hospital. En route to the hospital, medication was administered in an attempt to bring her out of this abnormally long febrile seizure. In the end, she was given too much: "Enough Ativan to knock out an adult male," my husband and I were told. As a result, her oxygen levels tanked and her heart rate dropped. During the utter chaos unfolding in the ambulance, I ended up holding an oxygen mask to her face that was almost bigger than her entire head as the paramedics scrambled to keep her alive.

Once in the emergency room, I witnessed the most painfully beautiful orchestra of medical personnel I've ever seen in my life. Nurses checked vitals, urgently directed orders, and then above the clamor I heard, "Respiratory failure; we need to intubate."

My husband had driven behind the ambulance, and because we were fighting five o'clock traffic, he got there a bit after us. He had put a freaking-out wife and seizing baby into the back of an ambulance and now arrived at the emergency room to find his child on a ventilator and his wife sitting on the cold tile floor while staring at the unfolding pandemonium. If you've never watched machines breathe for a tiny body, I absolutely do not recommend it. After the chaos had died down, I gingerly navigated the tubes and wires keeping my child alive and lay next to her in a bed five times her size while Jeremy talked to nurses and updated family. As tears ran down my face and into her sweet, matted hair, the only prayer I could choke out was "Please let me keep her." Six days later we walked out of the pediatric intensive care unit with a perfectly happy, very hungry Pacey Claire, a prescription for an anticonvulsant, and the warning that it might happen again. Even still, the doctors could not fathom how her body had withstood the overwhelming trauma from the seizure and the overdose, but I could. He had let me keep her.

In the months that followed, people often commented on how "okay" I seemed, how well I seemed to be taking this, and how unshaken I appeared by having almost lost my at-the-time only child. Of course, we had the most ideal outcome possible—a healthy, relatively unaffected child who walked and talked and played and breathed like any other little girl. And on the outside, I think I did seem okay. I wasn't curled in a ball on the couch or unable to go about our day-to-day activities.

But unseen by anyone else, I was spiraling on the inside. I was struggling to reconcile the God who let us keep her with the God who let this happen in the first place. I was in a constant state of fight-or-flight, ready for her to begin seizing at any given moment. I was the furthest thing from okay, but for the time I kept that to myself. I think it was a mixture of pride—I did not want anyone to see me as wounded, in need of time and love to heal—and an uncertainty of how to move forward, so I just . . . did.

What I didn't know then was this: Healing isn't linear. It isn't a straight shot. And when I tried to force it to follow a straight and narrow path, I just hindered the process and ended up back at the beginning. Six months after Pacey's seizure, six months into being "okay" and handling all of this so impressively, the trauma finally got its day on center stage. I had held it off for as long as I could, but the walls had given way to fear and flashbacks and I had nothing left. So on the cold, hard tile of our bathroom floor, I gave in to hours of rolling panic attacks. It was like all the pain of the last six months was exiting my body at once, and there was nothing I could do to stop it. The same thing happened the next day. And then the next. That is how I ended up on a therapist's very comfortable couch, desperately in need of tools to feel better. I knew I couldn't live like this anymore but didn't know where to start. So I said that. "I feel like I should be okay"—there was that word again—I told the therapist. "Pacey is fine and healthy. I'm the one who's not. I feel guilty for being such a mess, and I'm confused as to why I was able to hold it together for the last six months."

> HEALING ISN'T LINEAR. IT ISN'T A STRAIGHT SHOT. AND WHEN I TRIED TO FORCE IT TO FOLLOW A STRAIGHT AND NARROW PATH, I JUST HINDERED THE PROCESS AND ENDED UP BACK AT THE BEGINNING.

The therapist leaned in and asked, "But have you been?"

It felt like a scene from a movie where a person gets sucked through time and everything around them is moving at warp speed even as they stay the same. *Wait*, I asked myself. *Have I been okay this whole time? No. Definitely not. Not even a little bit.* Something clicked into place and I realized I'd been trying to fake it until I made it, which come to find out is not actually a Bible verse. Why had I done that? Why had I felt like I needed to do that? And how many other people were walking around doing the same?

Hint: I've since discovered that it's a lot. It doesn't even necessarily take a global pandemic to cause us to behave this way, but it sure didn't help. You don't have to be a parent or have walked through a particularly traumatic experience to be very much not okay while pretending that you are. You can have a stressful job, familial problems, or—heck—be trying to date in a time of swipe right or left.

Bleeding out and losing limbs, you and I often soldier forward because forward seems to be the only option and the show must go on. After all, we don't want those around us to be weighted by our pain. And so I wore my fake okay-ness as a badge of honor. Over time I found out I was not the only wearer of such a badge, and I was not the only member of the "Yeah, I'm okay" club. In reality, so many of us try to push away the creeping dark and doubt and to stuff down the dread and our screaming insides, all for the sake of being okay.

NOT FINE, ACTUALLY

Our need to appear okay is at war with the internal pain and fear, and eventually our inner world begins to crumble because the walls were never meant to hold that weight. We believe that the journey from hurt to healed is a straight line, a course from point A to point Z with no collateral damage, no steps backward, and no mess ups. And this belief system is killing us.

Unfortunately, this need to have it all together is often worse in the church. We are more than willing to pop an Advil when our back hurts, but when it comes to emotional distress, we have been taught to think things like *Well, I have Jesus, so I shouldn't need help with my thoughts, trauma, and inner pain.* We don't believe our mental state and health matter, and it shows. Like the culture around us, we prioritize achievement and physical appearance.

Fun fact: You can have a really craptastic mental state even while being skinny and at the top of your class. (I speak from experience.) It's just one more way the world has crept into our theology, and we must be diligent to root it out.

I will never understand the stigma that surrounds mental health care in the church. The weirdness toward therapy and even more so toward medication is one of my least favorite things about us Christians (second only to our self-righteous sin classification system). It's as though mental health doesn't matter, doesn't count, and certainly should not be talked about above a quiet whisper cloaked in the appropriate amount of shame. And we wonder why Christians are experiencing skyrocketing rates of suicide, divorce, and depression, just like the rest of the world.

According to the Anxiety and Depression Association of America, 40 million adults in the United States have anxiety disorders, making it the most prevalent mental illness in the country. These disorders are "highly treatable," but just 36.9 percent of people with serious anxiety are treated.[1] That's insane. Less than 40 percent of the 40 million people who have been through some traumatic event or who can't seem to get their brains to slow down ever get help, whatever that help may look like. Mental health issues can stem from genetics or environments, traumatic events or brain chemistry. You may have a natural disposition toward anxiety, and when something crazy happens, it tips the scale. At the end of the day, I don't think it matters all that much how you got into the boat you're in—what matters is that the boat is taking on water and if you don't get help, you're going to end up treading water for the rest of your life. I don't know about you, but my legs are not that strong.

So you have to figure out what getting help looks like for you, and you have to invite God in on the journey. For me, that journey has included therapy, medication (thank You, Jesus, for Prozac), and natural remedies like essential oils and breathing techniques. I've had to cut out caffeine completely and limit my sugar intake. I've found a workout I love while also taking time to rest and read fiction again. The prescription for your mental health will look different for you, so there is no copy and paste answer. It took time and work and trial and error for me to find the lineup of things that really helped me, and my best advice for finding yours would be to not think you have to land it all at once. You know yourself and likely know off the cuff what absolutely does not feel like self-care to you, but you also may surprise yourself. You could possibly stumble upon something like watercolor painting or long walks that calm your mind and later add in therapy or mindfulness practices. It doesn't have to be perfect and it doesn't need to all be figured out at once. It just needs to be a priority.

The good news is that God is in it. I mean, He's already there because He's everywhere and in everything, but we humans tend to have a penchant for trying to elbow God out of our mess when, in fact, the mess gets a whole lot less messy when we just put down our dukes and say, *Here it is God. All the mess, all the junk, all my humanness. Lead me in the way everlasting.* And then we get some help because God created scientists and therapists, dang it.

As I've said, for me, getting help started by going to weekly sessions with a therapist, digging out the lies I believed about my life and about God and replacing them with His truth. I realize now that one of the biggest reasons our journey to healing takes longer and is more painful than necessary is because we don't start at the root. Maybe the road wouldn't be so convoluted and confusing if we started at the beginning. So often we skip over the start, over the important foundational issues, and point our finger to a later point and say, "Here. Right here is where I want to start, with the issue at hand. Fix it. Fix me." But in reality, you and I need to start

twenty years ago when we first started believing we are alone in the world and therefore could not accept help.

If you don't start at the bottom of the tree, all you're going to be doing is hacking at limbs so big they'll tear you apart as they fall. You need to start by digging up the faulty lies that have taken root in your life. Then to ensure you aren't left with gaping holes waiting to snap an ankle the next time you walk by, you have to replace what had grown in the dark with the beautiful truth of God's Word. And then you have to keep coming back and packing down the earth where those holes used to be, reminding yourself of the finished work of the Cross and what that means for you, no matter what life throws your way.

There were three paramount lies that took me the most work to dig out: that God is not good, that I am solely responsible for myself, and that anxiety always and forever would be my lot in life. Week after week I sat on my therapist's couch and got back to work at digging up the latest lie we'd uncovered. We went deeper into why I believed what I believed, and all the while we were packing truth into the open ground.

THE LIES THAT KEEP US FROM HEALING

1. The lie: God is not good and does not want good things for me.

This one tends to creep up anytime something I deem "bad" happens. It's the "woe is me" version of *Why do bad things happen to good people?* And in a world that seems to be growing ever more dark, it's easy to slide into the negative frame of mind that God doesn't want good things for us. And if He doesn't want good things for us, then how could He be good?

The truth:

> Who among you, if his son asks him for bread, will
> give him a stone? Or if he asks for a fish, will give him a
> snake? If you then, who are evil, know how to give good
> gifts to your children, how much more will your Father in
> heaven give good things to those who ask him.
>
> MATTHEW 7:9-11

Think of anyone you love unconditionally. If they asked you for a sandwich, would you serve them up a nice plate of gravel? Or if they wanted some fresh salmon, would you give them a python? (I'm gagging as I type that, to be honest.) No. You wouldn't. And you are a human—someone separated from God before Christ came, now in Christ considered good and righteous, but still human. Hopefully you have some concept of how much greater God is than you, which should make clear how much more God wants to give you good things than you want to give them to those you love.

But what about the times you unknowingly ask for a python and graciously get salmon instead? Maybe you didn't know you asked for something that would serve as a serpent in your life, but guess who did? God. God's no is still better than the world's best yes, and believing that requires the kind of faith and hope that are only possible in Christ. Because sometimes God's no means the loss of a parent or the ending of a relationship you thought would last forever. Sometimes it feels like an unanswered prayer or (in our human experience) "nothing" happening. Those experiences require us to believe that we really do serve a God who is good, who works all things together for good for those who serve Him (see Romans 8:28), and that His definition of "good" far outreaches ours.

Even when those noes result in pain, hurt, and trauma, He is still in them. And in the moment they may hurt like crazy; no one is trying to deny that. But the great news is we serve a God with really big shoulders. He can carry your frustration, disappointment, and confusion. He is not adverse to your negative emotions. When you don't understand why things had to go the way they did, His goodness shines through all the more by His steadfastness. He doesn't leave your side even when you're screaming at the top of your lungs how much you hate Him for doing this to you (yes, I've done this). Not understanding His plan does not mean He doesn't have one, and it doesn't mean it isn't good, because He knows all, sees all, and understands all, and that's why it's called faith. If you're smack in the midst of feeling this way, read on—I've got some goodness for you.

2. The lie: I need to be able to do it all myself.

Pride is likely one of the biggest hindrances to our healing. You may be thinking, *I'm not prideful!* And maybe you're not proud in the traditional, puffed up, looking down your nose way. But pride can masquerade as humility quite easily, in the inability to accept help, believing you don't need it, or thinking you can, in fact, do all the healing (and generally all the things) on your own. The proverb "pride goes before destruction" (Proverbs 16:18, ESV) can be said about the haughty kind of pride we're accustomed to talking about. But I wholeheartedly believe quiet pride goes before destruction as well because we were never meant to go at it all alone.

The truth:

> Carry one another's burdens; in this way you will fulfill
> the law of Christ. For if anyone considers himself to be
> something when he is nothing, he deceives himself.
> GALATIANS 6:2-3

God created us for community, both with Him and with one another. And I am the first in line to admit that I do not always follow Paul's instruction to allow others to carry my burdens or to carry burdens for others. I am a lone wolf by nature, the woman who casually mentions that she and her husband had a conversation about divorce a few months ago to a friend who is shell-shocked to hear we are even struggling. It's not my finest character trait, and I'm thankful for Paul's clear direction here. I appreciate that he doesn't tell us to expect others to bear our burdens, but keeps the focus on how we can shoulder them for others, which is very on-brand for Paul. Maybe if we spent more time looking for the friends whose shoulders are sagging under the weight of life and walked arm in arm with them, our lives would feel a little less heavy.

And maybe if we didn't consider ourselves either above or not even worthy of another's help, we would have company on our journey to healing. When we refuse to receive help when someone reaches out to bear our burdens, not only are we doing ourselves a disservice, but we rob someone else of the opportunity to express the love of Christ within them. The examples of me robbing others of the ability to love me well are countless, unfortunately, from simple things like refusing help with the girls when work gets crazy to my incessant habit of walking through the hardest life seasons alone.

Right at the seven-year itch of our marriage, Jeremy and I hit a particularly rough season. We were busy and tired and disconnected, often functioning more like roommates than spouses, and things began to fall apart. It got so low we had legitimate conversations about whether we should attempt a trial separation (which never happened), and do you want to know how many people knew we were struggling at all? Zero. And that's not to say friends hadn't reached out, noticing I seemed particularly stressed/distant/anxious.

> **YOU ARE NOT A BURDEN; YOU HAVE BURDENS.**

I had chosen not to let them in because I thought I could shoulder it myself, and when I look back on that season, I can see how beneficial it would have been to have had help.

You don't have to go through life, healing, and hardships alone. You are not a burden; you have burdens. You have the Ultimate Burden Helper in Christ to help you along, but He wants you to allow others into your pain as well.

3. The lie: I'll always feel this way.

I have a tendency to speak in absolutes—*always, never, forever.* I wish I had this propensity when it comes to the positives, but it's more when I'm looking at things in a negative light.

> *This season of hardship is going to last forever.*
> *This struggle is never going to get any better.*
> *I'm always going to feel this way.*

And because the journey of healing is not linear—it's more like a squiggly line that gets lost and reappears—and because you rarely see the light at the end of the tunnel or even the next step, it's easy to believe that you will, in fact, always struggle with this burden and always feel the way you feel right now. Will these things forever be a part of your plight, like the thorn in Paul's side, which he describes in 2 Corinthians 12?

The truth:

> Therefore we do not give up. Even though our outer person is being destroyed, our inner person is being renewed day by day. For our momentary light affliction

is producing for us an absolutely incomparable eternal
weight of glory.

2 CORINTHIANS 4:16-17

Absolutely incomparable. Two of my favorite words in Scripture. To
fully understand the weight of these words in the life of the author,
Paul, you have to know what the man had gone through. Arrested
three times, shipwrecked three times, habitually separated from
his friends, whipped, beaten with rods, and stoned, the guy pretty
much took a beating his entire life.[2] And yet, with full confidence,
Paul was able to say that none of this even remotely compared to
the eternal glory we'll experience in heaven.

Our problem isn't that we think about our afflictions too much
or give them too much weight; it's that we think of the coming
weight of glory so little. None of this life compares to what is to
come! That doesn't take away from the hard things we experience
in this life; Paul was honest about his afflictions and cried out to
God to take them away. But I think the ace in Paul's pocket was
the knowledge that the scale was tipped toward glory. Maybe there
will always be remnants of past trauma in your life. Maybe your
struggles with anxiety won't miraculously dissipate (or maybe they
will). But the truth you can hold on to is that you won't always feel
this way because you won't always live in this body. And the best
way a believer can hold on to that truth in a world of darkness is to
keep their eyes on heaven, to hold eternity as the most important
thing, to remember that this life is a vapor and that the best parts
of it pale in comparison to the glory heaven holds.

I still have a lot of scars and pockmarks from Pacey's traumatic,
crazy-long seizure and its aftermath. I don't do well when either
of my kids get sick, even if it's just a severe runny nose. Every

heightened temperature transports me back to the PICU with all its wires and tubes. I have trouble hearing other people talk about medical trauma because it reminds me of my own. I still sometimes deal with survivor's guilt, an overwhelming feeling of annoyance with myself that I continue to struggle with this, seeing as we had the most ideal outcome. But now that I've let go of my need for healing to follow a straight line, the journey has gotten easier.

There is no formula or timetable you can follow to heal from past trauma and pain. If there were and I knew it, I'd be a millionaire. You must just put one foot in front of the other, trusting that the Father will catch you if (or when) you fall. And don't forget to look back at the squiggly line that is your healing to see all the ways His goodness and mercy have been evident throughout the journey.

Chapter 10

WHY AM I SO DANG TIRED?

There is virtue in work and there is virtue in rest.
Use both and overlook neither.
ALAN COHEN

REGARDLESS OF WHAT MY HUSBAND MAY SAY, I am not a hypochondriac. Sure, I may be well acquainted with WebMD and acutely attuned to my pulse, but a hypochondriac I am not. But I was 100 percent sure I was having a stroke not long ago.

Over the last two years of building a presence and business on the internet, I've had the blessing of putting together an incredible team of people with the same goal of bringing the gospel to others in an honest and authentic way. Expanding our team has allowed me to stop wearing all the hats. I mean, at one time, I wore every single one: podcaster, podcast manager, content creator, author, graphic designer, assistant, marketer. I still wear a lot of them, but I've gotten to hand many of them over to our beautiful, wildly talented team. Except for when I refuse to do so.

We had just completed the largest launch the Crappy Christian Co. has seen to date with the Collective—a paid membership group that allows our already awesome Instagram community to lean in a little closer. It had been a pipe dream ever since Crappy Christian's conception, a way to connect more intimately with our people, a safe place to talk about hard things, and a consistent income stream that offered to potentially take the business to the next level. The launch had more moving parts, more registrations, more everything than ever in our two years of business. We were also functioning with the largest team we'd ever had. You want to know who did every single part of that launch? Me.

And I do not say that proudly. I honestly don't even know what came over me, but what I do know is that I'd never been so exhausted in my life. Emotionally, physically, spiritually, and mentally, I was toast. Like, I had to pull over on the interstate so I didn't fall asleep driving level toast. It was not cute. So a few days after the launch, when the exhaustion really started to set in, my hands started tingling. And then one side of my face started to feel a little numb. Not to mention I couldn't keep my eyes open for more than a few hours. It was bad enough that my notoriously chill husband was concerned. I eventually spoke with a doctor friend, and he walked me through the exercises to determine if someone is having a stroke and decided I was not in fact having a stroke. My body was just exhausted.

So. Embarrassing. Why? Because I have spent a good deal of time curating content that centers around the idea of hustle culture being a liar and how to stay away from it. I have no less than four Instagram highlights devoted to teachings on the importance of not getting caught up in workaholism and choosing rest. I've done podcast series and been a guest on other shows on the subject. I mean, it's kind of my thing. And here I was: burned out, depleted, and googling "symptoms of a stroke." It's not like I didn't have help. I had three employees and a very hands-on husband who were ready and willing to do what they could. I even had friends offering to pitch in. But I thought I could do it better. Just goes to show that even those who are the loudest debunkers of a lie can fall for it again.

I believed that the success of my business and ministry hinged on this launch, that if I didn't work as hard as humanly possible, it would fail and therefore I would fail. And for a minute I believed the biggest, grossest lie the hustle tells: that in this moment, my worth was dependent on how hard I worked. So I worked like crazy. Leading up to launch day, I got up at 5 a.m. to start working on sales copy and marketing materials and back-end software stuff. I would take off an hour to run car pool, be back at work for three hours, go do a crazy strenuous eight hundred calorie work-out, come back to work, do car pool, and then work on the launch until 11 p.m. Rinse and repeat for about eleven days. I was just as delightful as you think I was.

The launch itself went great and was very successful. But I didn't really get to enjoy it, much less keep my eyes open. I was snippy with my family, dragging myself out of bed, and had generally lost my luster for life, just going through the motions required of me. But I think the worst part was hearing from my team. Days after the launch was finished I checked in with my communications manager, who lovingly shared that she wished she could have been more a part of the last week. Hearing that she had felt boxed out of this huge moment in company history, had felt uninformed, and that she couldn't do her job well because she didn't know what was going on came down like a convicting hammer on my already tired brain. I had messed up and I knew it. It was like all at once all the lies I was believing dissolved and I was left holding exhaustion in one hand and regret in the other.

Apologizing for my responsibility in leaving her and the rest of my team out was one of the easiest apologies I've ever given.

It wasn't my heart and certainly wasn't my plan to make them feel uninvolved, but I had. I didn't set out to do it all myself and not let anyone help. I got ahead of myself, distracted by the glitter of success. I bought a lie. Because here's the deal: How you respond in highly stressful situations is usually a pretty good indicator of what you believe and how you function in your day to day. So when I responded to stress by overworking, overstressing, preventing people from helping, and believing I had to do it all, it's fair to say I was, to some degree, proving that I function that way normally. And I did. Looking back at that season I see more than a little stress, not enough sleep, and a person who generally wasn't taking care of herself.

> HOW YOU RESPOND IN HIGHLY STRESSFUL SITUATIONS IS USUALLY A PRETTY GOOD INDICATOR OF WHAT YOU BELIEVE AND HOW YOU FUNCTION IN YOUR DAY TO DAY.

The unimportance of rest is one of hustle culture's headlining lies. Like if hustle culture were a band, working yourself into the ground would be where the show really hits its stride. I know this because my original wake-up call out of overwork coincided with being diagnosed with adrenal failure. This most recent crash and burn is not your girl's first rodeo, unfortunately. And this is why I talk about the hustle being such a smooth talker and great liar. I know how it deceives and I *still* fell for it! I slipped into believing the old lies that I couldn't succeed if I didn't work like crazy and that my worth was tied up in the success of this launch. I cannot emphasize this enough: Just because you know something's untrue doesn't mean you can't ever fall for it again. Life and knowledge are not straight lines; the human experience is always morphing and we are always growing. I'm proof that even teachers and leaders are susceptible to picking up what the world is putting down.

Here's the truth: I could've gotten through a big, stressful launch without being exhausted and convinced I was having a stroke. I could have welcomed my team into the inner workings and let them do their jobs. I could've asked my husband for more help, both in the business and in the home. I could've taken naps and nights off, held the launch with an open hand, and believed God would light my path and lead the way. I could've trusted my Father instead of my own ability. I had every opportunity to practice what I preach and stay out of the hustle, but I didn't. So here we are. Now what?

RECOVERY BEGINS WITH REST

I could spend the next few months beating myself up, burdened by guilt, apologizing to my team over and over, looking back at all the ways I messed it up. Or I could rest, get back on my feet, and begin moving forward in the truth. I had to figure out what kind of rest I needed in order to get the best rest I could and get back in the game.

Fun fact: There is more than one type of rest. There are in fact seven—physical, mental, sensory, creative, emotional, social, and spiritual. Lucky for you, I needed all seven following the launch and several times since, so I am well versed in them.

Physical. You probably know if you're physically exhausted. You can't keep your eyes open, you keep yawning, you don't have the energy to do small tasks. Although I experienced these around launch day, I felt the signs of physical exhaustion most acutely when I was training for a marathon because an author I liked told me in her book that I should become a runner, and your girl doesn't do anything halfway. I don't like to run. With my short legs and stocky frame, I am not built for long distances. I'm more of a "pick up heavy things and put them down" kind of girl. But there I was, hitting the pavement every single day on a rigorous training plan because someone I looked up to had convinced me that the road to success is apparently an actual marathon.

I got all the way up to ten miles before my body said, *That is absolutely enough*, and wouldn't let me run anymore. With shin splints, aching arches, popping knees, and general, chronic exhaustion, I gave up my short-lived dream of being a marathoner and went on to find a workout that I actually love, one that feeds my body rather than depletes it and that I anticipate doing rather than dread. I also go to bed early enough to earn myself the coveted "Mawmaw" nickname amongst friends.

What this can look like: Take naps when you can. Put down your phone and go to bed at a reasonable time. Don't pick up physical activities that don't make you feel good either during or after. Take care of your body so that you can keep showing up, keep serving others, and keep loving your people well.

Mental. Welcome to the digital era, the age of mental exhaustion. You know you're mentally exhausted if you've been reading the same word for ten minutes, you can't remember things as sharply as usual, and maybe you even get a little extra judgy and cranky. Because I create content for a living, I'm required to be online and connected much of the time, which makes me extra susceptible to mental exhaustion. So I have had to put strong boundaries and practices in place that allow me mental rest.

One of the best things to come out of the quarantine of 2020 was the reminder of how much I love to read fiction. Like, I love it. It helps me chill out and even check out, escaping into another world for a little bit and preparing me to come back to the real one a little more ready to take it on.

What this can look like: You have to discover what provides that mental rest and make time to do it. Maybe reading is your thing or perhaps it's mindful meditation. You might just need some quiet time alone to reset your mind, or you could even get engrossed in a puzzle. If you're mentally wiped day in and day out, it's going to be extremely difficult to work unto the Lord and use your gifts for the glory of the Kingdom, so protect that asset like all the others!

Sensory. This is actually one of the most prevalent forms of exhaustion today. With all the lights, screens, and loud noises, your senses are probably on constant overload, keeping you living in a state of overwhelm. As someone with high-functioning anxiety, I know that sensory overload kills me. I have two awesome but loud kids and I make my living on the very noisy internet. My full-time job is basically to share and listen to opinions while my kids climb all over me and yell about who had the last cookie. You know what? I love it. Until I don't. Until the lights and the sounds and the touching and, ugh, the smells get to be too much and I feel like my brain is going to snap. I know I need sensory rest when my husband's breathing makes me want to send a remote control flying in his direction.

Sensory rest takes a lot of self-control. It requires you to unplug both literally and figuratively. Sometimes I just need to crawl into bed while my phone is on the other side of the house and take a minute to be inaccessible. I'm not above locking myself in the bathroom for ten minutes so no one can touch me. I've learned that taking care of my senses has to be a priority because if I don't, I can find it difficult to hear from the Lord. Not because He isn't speaking, but because I'm so overwhelmed, I can't hear Him. An easy way to fix that is to get still and quiet the noise around me.

What this can look like: We're big fans of tech-free days at our house—no phones, tablets, TV, nothing. You may decide to soothe your senses by putting in earplugs, taking a bath, reading an actual book, or getting a massage. If nothing else, don't look at a screen for an hour before bed and see if you sleep more easily!

Creative. If your work requires you to innovate, you might be creatively exhausted. When you get paid to turn out unique content of any form, the creative drive can begin to be depleted. One of my dearest friends is an incredible calligrapher. I could watch her write words all day. Actually, during that launch I mentioned at the beginning of this chapter, I had her hand-letter the name of every person who signed up and taped them to the wall of my office as a reminder that I don't have to do it alone. I did so selfishly, just so I could watch her do it.

One Christmas season she made gorgeous hand-lettered ornaments that went viral on the internet and landed her hundreds and hundreds of orders. I remember talking to her when the final order went out and her saying something along the lines of "I never want to letter another thing ever again." She was completely creatively exhausted. The thing she loves to do had lost its luster because she had been required to do it so much.

What she needed was creative rest. To get out in nature and away from her work. She needed to put down her pen for a little while to let those creative muscles take a break. And so she did. She focused on her home and went on weekend trips with her husband. Soon the desire to letter and create came creeping back in (and I totally did not tell her, "I told you so").

It's likely that you flex your creativity more than you think. You don't need to be an artist to create; every time you come up with an idea or solution, you're depleting your creativity. And when you're exhausted in this area, it can be really hard to keep showing up in the spaces God has placed you in.

What this can look like: First of all, taking a break from whatever requires you to create is the best creative rest you can give yourself. To be replenished, you may just need to be outside for a little while, spending time with the ultimate Creator. You might seek out someone else's creativity and revel in their ability. Or you could experiment with something new and different you've been thinking about trying out.

Emotional. Whether or not you consider yourself "emotional," you are a multifaceted human being with feelings and experiences that impact you in some capacity every single day. We're all in a constant state of letting out emotion and taking on those of the people around us. That can be especially wearing if we are particularly empathetic, as I have learned from watching my former boss. She is the most servant-hearted person I've ever met. In the few years I've known her, she has delivered more meals, cleaned more dishes, made more gifts, and bought more coffee for others than anyone I've ever known. The outpouring of her love for Jesus and people honestly comes naturally for her. I've also witnessed her generosity come back and bite her in the butt, especially when it's never reciprocated. She'll admit she's not great at letting people take care of her, and more than once I've had to strong-arm my way into taking care of her when she's down. But I've also sat across from her as she fought through tears of just feeling like she didn't have any more to give. Gently I've told her, "You have got to start saying no."

Whether you're a never-say-no-er or not, learning to protect your emotional space is imperative if you are to function from a place of rest.

My mom has told me my whole life, "No is a full sentence." It does not always require explanation or excuses. Sometimes you have to say no to good things so that you can keep showing up. If you say yes to everything, you may be picking up good things that aren't yours to carry. Instead, practice discernment. Surround yourself with people who will force you to let them love you. And trust that the most excellent yes is one that is given freely.

What this can look like: Guarding your calendar so it doesn't get overfilled is a great way to start protecting your emotional load, a first step into the world of ever-important boundaries. And while we're talking about boundaries, there may be times when you need to step away from being all things to all people so that you avoid emotional burnout and are able to be anything to anyone when it matters most.

Social. You know that moment when you've been around people just a few minutes too long and you start to crash? Listen, this isn't exclusive to introverts; even more naturally extroverted people can begin to feel weighed down by social interaction. Upon first glance, I present as an extrovert. Because I'm gregarious and funny, almost always the first one on the dance floor, most people assume I'm an extrovert. But the truth is, my social tank is smaller than a pregnant woman's bladder. I have crazy low tolerance for being around people, and after an especially full weekend I often go into hermit mode. I answer no text messages, don't open Instagram, and refuse to step outside of my home. I retreat because I know what will happen if I keep going at this same social pace. I will check out. Physically, I'll be there. But mentally I will have stopped listening to your story ten minutes ago. I get moody and cranky, and my ability to be a decent human being just bottoms out.

We are more accessible and available than ever before, now that our social interactions spill over into the solitude of our homes via social media. Here's the truth, though—there's only so much of you to go around. Don't you want your people to get the good stuff, not just the dredges left over when you've exhausted yourself by showing up and saying yes to everything? Even Jesus spent time in solitude to recharge and reconnect with the Father, so I think it's a good example to follow.

What this can look like: Rather than waiting until you're at the point of social exhaustion, maybe you need to carve out time in your schedule each week to be alone with the Father consistently. Or it could be you need to maintain better boundaries with what and who you're allowing into your life, both in real time and virtually. Or perhaps you just need to get better at saying no, which seems to be an overarching theme here!

Spiritual. I'd venture a guess that most of us need spiritual rest—that "lie down in green pastures" kind of feeling where you just fall back into the promises and goodness of God. Where you cease striving and just know that He is God. I know I need spiritual rest when God feels far away. When I feel unanchored and lonely and lose sight of my purpose, I know it's time to get quiet and spend time with the Lord. This has happened to me a few times after particularly difficult friendship seasons when I've been left hurt or betrayed, feeling like I can't trust anyone. I've allowed those feelings to bleed over into my relationship with God, even though He never has and never will do any of those things that caused the bleeding. It also happens in busy seasons when I don't prioritize spending intentional time in the Word. The fastest track to spiritual exhaustion for me is not starting my day with Jesus. When I'm left to power through the day with only my own energy and efforts, let me tell you, both are lacking.

What this can look like: Some days I get to 3 p.m., only to realize I am just absolutely white-knuckling the way through my day, stressed out for no real reason and feeling a bit like a woman on an island. And 9.9 times out of 10 it's because I haven't been talking to Jesus, not as a discipline but as a practice that keeps me anchored to truth. Great news alert: You don't have to do anything to get "back" in communion with Jesus. Even though you may have gotten distracted, He never left. A pastor once told me that reconnecting with Jesus is as simple as turning your eyes back on His face, and He's quick to meet you right where you are. It's worth mentioning that when life feels less heavy and your heart less weary, there are so many benefits to be found in engaging in a community of believers and making time for the spiritual disciplines that are meant for our benefit and closeness to Christ. But for those seasons when it's all you can do to be in conversation with Him through the day, that's enough too.

You may need one or more of these seven types of rest at any point in life, interchangeably and at varying degrees of necessity. But they're always present and available, practices that can be interwoven into our daily lives.

Hopefully, just by reading through this chapter you can more easily identify what kind of rest you're in need of, but the trick will be actually taking time to care for yourself. After the successful but exhausting launch of the Crappy Christian Collective, my primary rest needs came roaring to the forefront—physical, emotional, social. These are the forms of rest I'm nearly always in need of, but in especially stressful and busy seasons it's obvious to everyone around me that I'm completely spent. As a recovering hustle-aholic, slowing down is difficult for me, but when I'm stressed and exhausted I have a really difficult time looking like Jesus. Sincerity and attentiveness go out the window, and it's difficult to be a witness of Christ's love when you just generally don't care what another person is saying. Was it not better for me to take a minute and recover than to just keep trucking through, running on empty? I took naps, read fiction, fiercely guarded my calendar, and allowed myself to get back on my feet before jumping back into the fray. I may not have wanted to take the time "off," but I knew myself well enough to know I needed to and that if I didn't, things would likely get ugly.

In such moments, self-care is the furthest thing from selfish. It's also the fastest way to fill back up so that we can continue serving others well.

Chapter 11

MY CHURCH HURT ME;
NOW WHAT?

When you let people put you up on a pedestal,
you step one step in any direction, and you're going to go down.

JAMES DOBSON

I STARTED ATTENDING CHURCH willingly when I was nineteen. Up until that point I had just gone along with my parents on Sundays, largely going through the motions of Christianity. But after a few wild months away from home, I realized I actually wanted to be in the community of other believers. This proved to be quite easy, considering I attended a large university in southern Louisiana, smack in the heart of the Bible Belt.

During the second semester of my freshman year, I started showing up for the evening college church service at a church near campus and, honestly, I loved it. The worship was awesome, the teaching was dynamic, and I was enough of a baby Christian that I wasn't really concerned about theology. Not only that, but this college ministry had thriving community groups and offshoots and approximately a million ways to get involved. So I did. I quickly started serving within the ministry and began making friends. I felt as if I belonged and had a purpose. My relationship with Christ began to thrive.

About a year into my time there, some red flags began to appear in regard to the leader of the college ministry. At first I had seen him as an energetic and intense personality, but I became more uncomfortable with the side jokes about girls and women during his sermons. I wondered if they were indicative of how he actually viewed the other sex—seeing them as less than and often in his way. I started to think that maybe he wasn't the wildly dynamic pastor I'd thought he was. Maybe I even needed to be wary of him.

A lot of church hurt and trauma starts like that. Red flags and questionable characteristics begin to reveal themselves, and while you may not feel empowered to do anything about it, you might take a step back from the leader and ministry team. Because that's the thing about leadership, isn't it? Those closest to them often pick up some of the leader's attributes, good or bad. In my case, I began putting physical and emotional distance not only between myself and the leader but most of his closest followers. Actually, I put distance between all of them but one.

I had caught the eye of a particularly cute and well-known leader within the college ministry. This was the first time I ever liked a boy who loved Jesus. In high school I'd had a penchant for the bad boys. But once I'd turned my life over to the Lord, I was determined to make my faith a part of my dating life as well.

I enjoyed spending time with him and felt comfortable around this guy. Once he took me on a mountain biking date and still wanted to be seen in public with me after I'd eaten dirt, not once but twice, while attempting to navigate a bike (something I was already awful at) over mountain terrain. We weren't serious, and I was absolutely fine with that. I simply had one request: I didn't want to kiss him until we were dating exclusively. Before committing to my faith, I'd done the casual hookup thing and it had grown stale. I was finally taking my sexuality and body seriously, and I had decided to start by setting this boundary. I didn't want to engage in any kind of physical intimacy with someone unless we were serious enough to be exclusive. Then came the test.

One night while we were watching TV, he asked if he could kiss me. Oh man, did I ever want him to kiss me. But I told him no. We obviously weren't serious (again, this was fine), so I really wanted to stick to the boundary I'd set. And yet he leaned in and very gently kissed me. I just sat there looking at him and thinking, *People don't tell you no, do they?*

The relationship didn't make it past that point; I was annoyed, and I think he was as well. There was no real animosity; just two people frustrated with each other and going their separate ways. Actually, if memory serves, I got the ole faithful "I think you've gotten the wrong idea about us" line. Which was startling because I had assumed boys who loved Jesus would be better than boys who didn't. Sadly, this was my first lesson in the truth that they can, in fact, sometimes be worse.

But the real problem was that this particular boy was very popular within the college ministry I'd been attending faithfully and it seemed he had gotten his pride hurt a little bit. I've never gotten direct confirmation about this, but it felt like the leader of the college ministry knew what had transpired, and I became a bit of a pariah. This would eventually culminate with him yelling at me for daring to speak over him after he had interrupted me. In front of a group of people. Quite loudly. It was awful.

I was shocked, appalled, and embarrassed. I never showed up to another ministry event or service. It had been a slow descent from being the golden girl who was *kind of* dating one of the golden boys into public humiliation, all because I had dared to hold a boundary with said boy (although I'm sure it wasn't quite spun that way). I walked away from that experience making one promise to myself: *I will pay attention to the red flags from here on. Whenever someone begins to show me who they are, I'm going to do my best to believe what I see the first time.* I didn't know what that would look like, but I was pretty sure I would find out at some point.

Not long after this I found another church with a college ministry that I got involved in, not quite wounded enough to swear off church altogether. I found a place I loved, met my husband there, enmeshed my life into its culture, and made all my friends within its walls. Not only were Jeremy and I married by the lead pastor, we were both baptized in that church. We had been members for seven years before I had to keep the promise I had made with myself to pay attention to red flags. The long and short of it was that my husband and I, along with a few other members, were accused by a fellow church member of something we simply hadn't done. And then our accuser was given the pulpit at a church meeting to air their issues in a highly unhealthy manner. Have you ever left a public place because you were so emotional you simply could not stay in your seat anymore? I have. And it sucks. We stood up and walked out of the meeting in the middle of it. We were lucky: After a few meetings with the leadership, we received immediate and sincere apologies.

LESSONS LEARNED THE HARD WAY

I learned a few lessons from the hurtful experiences I suffered at church. So many of us who have been wounded by that institution never thought we'd be here. We were taught to feel safe and vulnerable within those four walls. We were told that the leadership was worthy of our trust and could be safely followed. Also, not all issues show themselves out the gate. Some do, and we can still miss those. But time after time I hear people beat themselves up for getting hurt by their church. It's as if they believe they should have seen it coming, and yet they had spent years building trust and relationship with their leaders. It's easy to be blindsided once you've let your guard down in what you assumed was a safe haven.

Unfortunately, things tend to get sticky when we try talking about the hurt we've experienced. This is when we are often hushed. Pushed off to the side so that we don't cause a ruckus. Told that we are wholly the problem because the pastor (or other leader) is untouchable.

Not only that, but I want to take a moment to recognize how rare it is for a church to make amends, as ours quickly did. Our hurt was not further perpetuated by pride and the haughty belief that the leadership was incapable of messing up. They instantly recognized that they had misjudged the situation and actually put us in circumstances that were bound to cause wounds.

Even so, for my husband and me, the damage had been done. The curtain had been pulled back and this event had revealed deep-seated issues that were not only problematic, but that had not been seen that way by the leaders. After lots of prayer and many conversations between Jeremy and me and with our two closest friends, we made the difficult decision to leave the church that had helped build our marriage and our relationships with Christ. We left behind people we had considered friends for years and grieved when many of them watched us leave without speaking another word to us.

Leaving the safety and comfort of that church was one of the hardest things I've ever done. We essentially left behind everything that had once felt familiar because we sensed that the Lord was telling us to leave. When I look back on that season, I remember immense amounts of loneliness and confusion. How could something that was supposed to look so much like our Father have hurt us so much? What we were supposed to do now?

After our shared negative experience with a church, my husband and I grappled with the idea of joining another church, another group of humans who are flawed and imperfect and will thus be flawed and imperfect. But we knew in our hearts that our place was amongst believers; that our shared humanity shouldn't be enough to keep us away. There isn't a doubt in my mind that moving to another church was the right move for our family. We don't carry regret or shame about our decision, and we hold no ill will toward the people we left behind. But that's because as we were in the midst of it, we did a lot of work to make sure we didn't end up jaded and skeptical of any and all church leadership. We talked intimately with our pastors before we left, sharing the good, bad, and ugly of our decision. We dug into Scripture and allowed the Word to remind us of the importance of community. We asked those close to us to join us in praying about what our next steps were. It took effort and time to navigate a difficult situation well, but it was so worth it.

During my lifetime, and particularly during the ten-plus years I've walked closely with Christ, I have experienced life under many different leaders, both good and bad. The truth is, I likely wouldn't be writing this book if we hadn't found the church we now call home, where we are guided by faithful teachers and leaders. I would trust my life to some of these pastors; they have earned full permission to speak into the dark, hard parts of me. These are people who, while human, have worn the mantle of pastor well and done the title full justice.

Yet as you now know, my previous church experience was not a positive one. I've never shared about it publicly. It's likely that you have been through something similar. Because according to the church, the hurt we experience there should never be aired in public. It belongs in the dark, not talked about. Just go away and lick your wounds; you'll be fine because . . . Jesus.

And that I have a problem with. Because stuffing church hurt results in bitter, jaded Christians—believers who (often understandably) cannot separate the offense from the offender and thus just walk away from church altogether. Perhaps you haven't told your story because you still love some of the people in leadership who hurt you. Perhaps it's just too much, still too difficult to mention, and you find yourself unsure of where to even start to unpack the pain caused by the people you thought would protect you. I've been there—so burned by the institution that I could not fathom returning through its doors. I don't blame those who have left church because of the way they were treated, but I am sad that they miss out on being in community with the body of Christ. And I do believe that if we talked about it, if we felt safe to bring our church hurt to the surface, if we knew we could process what had happened, then maybe fewer people would find themselves isolated from the place that God intended to be our refuge.

Scripture is so clear about the importance of the body of Christ and our meeting together (and also about how to treat one another—I'm not saying the two are mutually exclusive).

> Let us consider how we may spur one another on toward
> love and good deeds, not giving up meeting together,
> as some are in the habit of doing, but encouraging
> one another—and all the more as you see the Day
> approaching.
> HEBREWS 10:24-25, NIV

From the moment God looked at Adam and saw it was not good for him to be alone, He intended for us to be in community. The book of Acts—in fact, the entire New Testament—shows how the early church exemplified what it looks like to come together for teaching and the breaking of bread, which facilitated wonders and belief throughout the people.

God created the body of Christ to function together but differently, and He's given each of us gifts that further the Kingdom. So when we take the pain someone has inflicted upon us and assume it comes from the institution as a whole, we not only do ourselves a disservice, we miss out on His design. God's intention is always good, and His intention for us is community.

WHEN LEADERS HURT US

To be clear, there are so many good men and women in church leadership. The call to ministry is a heavy one, often full of sacrifice and servanthood, little thanks, and a lot of incoming flak. Congregants hurt pastors, too, and often our leaders have an even more difficult time navigating that hurt from a "set apart" place of authority. The human element of church and community will always be messy.

Scripture is very clear about the standards church leaders should be held to. They're called to be above reproach, faithful, self-controlled, worthy of respect, and much more (see 1 Timothy 3). But I think we often forget that church leaders, like us, are still flawed humans living in a broken world. Like us, they have their own baggage and wounds, and they're navigating their own relationships and issues. Normal human failings coupled with a position of authority can create a whole lot of problems—from narcissism and unchecked power to a refusal to be questioned. And when an attitude of superiority begins to bubble up from within the spirit of a church leader, church hurt is inevitable.

In other words, we hold our leaders to a moral standard they won't always reach. This doesn't mean that they aren't wrong or that their actions aren't sinful, nor does grace demand that we give them a pass for bad behavior. Abuse should be addressed swiftly and directly; it should never be tolerated or brushed under the rug simply because it comes from a place of authority. But maybe it's time we stop idolizing leaders and instead practice gratitude for their gifts while recognizing that they are human too.

I am thankful and blessed that, despite being hurt twice by church leaders, I can look back and see that the enemy was never able to use the wrongs of others to steer me away from my Father. Because I think that's what Satan tries to do. He takes such offenses, no matter how big or small, and attempts to make them a wedge that comes between believers and the church, just when hurt Christians most need godly, loving people around them.

HEALING FROM CHURCH HURT

So how can we beat the enemy at his own game? How can we lean into Jesus and reach for healing rather than bitterness when the church gets it wrong? Here are some things that have worked for me:

1. Welcome Jesus in.

> We do not have a high priest who is unable to sympathize with our weaknesses, but one who has been tempted in every way as we are, yet without sin. Therefore, let us approach the throne of grace with boldness, so that we may receive mercy and find grace to help us in time of need.
> HEBREWS 4:15-16

I have a lot of favorite things about Jesus. Honestly, all of them. But high up on the list is the truth that He understands every single thing I experience or feel. Even when I struggle to believe that He is for me, I still know that it's true. And if Jesus understood anything, it's the pain of hurt and betrayal by religious figures. Hello, that's kind of how He ended up on a cross. So don't

> IF JESUS UNDERSTOOD ANYTHING, IT'S THE PAIN OF HURT AND BETRAYAL BY RELIGIOUS FIGURES.

believe the lie that Jesus can't understand or walk through church hurt with you and instead lay all your hurt and pain at His feet. There is no one more qualified to help you through this disappointment than Him. The reality is that Jesus is already in the situation with you, but the sooner you quit white-knuckling your pain and open your hands to receive His healing, the sooner you can move forward.

2. Take time off.

He makes me lie down in green pastures, he leads me beside quiet waters, he refreshes my soul.

PSALM 23:2-3, NIV

After both of my less than stellar experiences with church, what I needed most was time to rest and to allow Jesus to restore my soul from the beating it'd taken. This verse from Psalm 23 radically impacted my life then, as it has many other times. After the most recent hurt, my husband and I knew we needed to get plugged in to a church because it was important for our kids, but we committed not to serve for a full year. No nursery duty, no picking up chairs—we simply showed up, were poured into, and got to know our new church home.

If you've been hurt by the church, you may need to take some time off from even attending a service, and that's okay too. God is capable of meeting and communing with you from anywhere and never requires a brick-and-mortar building. What your soul needs to rest and heal is between you and Jesus. Before you can discern what God has next for you, you need time to process what happened to you.

3. But don't become an island.

Where two or three are gathered together in my name, I am there among them.

MATTHEW 18:20

Rest, recover, and allow your sweet Father to restore the things humans have taken from you. But do not do it as an island. Do not walk through the pain and try processing it alone. My husband and I didn't do a great job of this. Yes, we were back in community with believers soon after we'd been hurt, but out of a desire to protect our previous church, we didn't talk about it much outside of the safety of our marriage. Looking back, I wish we would have welcomed a few more trusted friends into the experience with us, to get different perspectives and also to allow them to pray and support us as we moved forward. Friends we knew would hear us with compassionate hearts and still be able to extend grace to those who had hurt us. People who would have helped steer us toward healing and forgiveness, avoiding bitterness and shame.

A couple of caveats: Of course, there's a difference between gossiping to sow discord and processing to find healing. It's important, though, not to allow fear of the former to keep you from the latter. Second, if you've experienced abuse (sexual or otherwise) at the hands of church leadership, please consider seeking the counsel of a professional to help you navigate the deep hurt, trauma, and betrayal.

4. Find new community.

Do not fear, for I am with you; do not be afraid, for I am your God. I will strengthen you; I will help you; I will hold on to you with my righteous right hand.

ISAIAH 41:10

"I will strengthen you; I will help you"—empowerment straight from the Father Himself. I really do believe that it grieves God when the leaders of the church hurt His kids. I also believe His perfect plan for us is to be in community with one another, functioning as a body with different gifts and abilities. And I think it makes the enemy extremely happy when church hurt keeps us from that. So once you've begun processing the pain, I encourage you to find a body of believers to join if you haven't yet done so. And if you're technically going to church but you're not really invested there, I encourage you to lean in so that you can begin investing in others and getting involved again at some point.

The church as an institution should be a place where we feel safe and protected. When instead we are hurt there, disillusionment is all but inevitable. Because of the grace and comfort we find in Jesus, however, we don't need to stop from functioning in community with our fellow believers. Church hurt is real, and the fallout is hard, horrible, and hurtful. Thankfully, our God is bigger still.

Chapter 12

WHY ARE CHRISTIANS SO WEIRD ABOUT SEX?

Don't get it twisted. Just because you are celibate does not mean
you are pure. Being in love with Jesus makes you pure.

UNKNOWN

AS A PRODUCT OF THE PURITY CULTURE, the *I Kissed Dating Goodbye* era, the days of True Love Waits and purity rings, it may come as a surprise to you that one of my favorite things to talk about is sex. Not in a graphic, gratuitous way; I'm not a frat boy, okay? But I do love to talk about such things as purity culture, sexuality, and married sex. In part because it makes people uncomfortable and I whole-heartedly believe that a lot of truth and freedom are on the other side of our comfort zone. I'm not trying to play the part of a shock jock; I don't have any interest in discussing sex and sexuality in the offhanded way the world tends to. What I am interested in is setting people free of shame and making sure we all know and understand what Scripture says about every facet of our lives—sex included.

And this, I'm afraid, is another area where some churches have wounded young people—even if it took years for the damage to appear. It's long past time for the church to step up and join the conversation about "taboo" topics because here's the reality: These things are going to be talked about one way or another. Why shouldn't the church be the leading voice when we do, in fact, have the corner on godly wisdom and discernment? I'm tired of feeling disqualified from conversations about hard things because I follow the way of Christ. Christians belong in the sexuality conversation because we serve the God who created sex, but instead we're often the ones shying away from talking about it at all.

If you didn't grow up in purity culture, let me paint a picture for you. Imagine that scene from *Mean Girls* where the PE coach who can't control the volume of his voice tells the students not to ever have sex because they will get chlamydia and die, but add some Jesus talk in there. In the simplest terms, as a teen, the lesson I took from purity culture was that Christians are to remain completely and utterly sexless (have no sexual thoughts, feelings, or actions) until they are married, and if they fail to achieve said sexlessness, they are headed straight to hell. Do not pass go, do not collect $200.

I'll never forget the first time I realized something was really wrong with the way I was being taught about sex by the church. The summer after I turned fourteen, I went to my first sleepaway camp with our youth group. The hardship of enduring a full week of camp food and sleeping with no AC was offset by the Blob. If you've never had the pleasure of attending summer camp, let me introduce you to it. The Blob is a gigantic inflatable that sits in a lake. You jump off a dangerously high deck directly onto it. As you land, the camper who jumped ahead of you (and now sits near the front of the Blob) is flung into the air like a rag doll. You watch that person catapult into water of questionable safety as you scooch forward and wait for the person behind you to jump on the

Blob and launch you into the air. It's really delightful and a highly anticipated part of the whole camp experience.

Before we left for camp we were given a packing list. Females were told to bring a one-piece bathing suit and knee-length shorts. Now at the time I didn't envision pairing the two together, but upon arriving at camp quickly discovered that both would in fact be worn together to Blob, swim, and kayak. That was fine with me; I was just excited to see how high I could fly.

When the first full day of camp rolled around, I got in line at the Blob behind a boy, who I realized wasn't wearing a shirt. I glanced at the guy behind me and noticed that he wasn't wearing a shirt either. None of the boys were wearing shirts. *Wait, hold up. Why am I wearing basketball shorts that my mom had to buy at Walmart specifically for this trip while the boys are SHIRTLESS?* I was suddenly aware of how sweaty and sticky I was, covered in one of those athletic one-piece swimsuits you wear for swim team to keep everything in place with knee-length basketball shorts over that.

After what seemed like hours of jumping into the lake, the shorts weighed approximately one hundred pounds, and I constantly had to hike them back into place as they slid down my slick bathing suit. The whole situation was very uncomfortable, exacerbated by the fact that the people with a Y chromosome were comfortable as could be. So after I had had my fill of the water, I sat down next to a female camp counselor in matching basketball shorts. I asked her why we had to wear so many clothes to swim and the boys didn't.

"Modest is hottest," she replied.

"Well, yeah, okay, but what's modest about being shirtless?" I asked. She was momentarily stumped, but it didn't take her long to regurgitate the standard youth group response: "Because it's our job as girls to make sure the boys don't stumble."

I wasn't strong enough in my faith then to see this statement for what it was, a foundational building block of purity culture. Once back home, it didn't take long for me to notice this same theme pop up whenever sexuality was a topic within youth group meetings. When we were spilt into girl and boy groups and talked to about sexuality, girls got the "modest is hottest" conversation while the boys got the "just don't have sex" one. The girls got the "boys will be boys" and the guys got the "boys will be boys" talk. The boys were taught that their minds were evil while the girls were taught that our bodies were the problem.

I remember a speaker once using the metaphor of a car: A "pure" woman was like a new shiny Corvette while an "impure" one—someone who had been intimate before marriage—was like a used car that everyone had already driven and honestly wasn't worth much anymore. Our teacher's intention, of course, was to keep us abstinent, but what they also succeeded in doing was completely messing up our view of ourselves and of sex.

I really do believe the people who spread this message mostly had good intentions. It's likely that the youth pastors and leaders and therefore the churches who picked up the purity culture narrative didn't set out to sexually cripple a generation—they just wanted us to understand the consequences that come with sexual intimacy outside of marriage. Over and over we were cautioned to keep our virginity intact until we were married, but no one ever told us how or why it even mattered to God.

By the early nineties, the purity culture message began to gain steam when the Southern Baptist Convention began its "True Love Waits" campaign, promoting sexual abstinence among youth through conferences, concerts, and purity pledges. Others joined the movement, and the more extreme versions of these events went even further than the abstinence message, teaching that women were to be appropriately submissive. We were not to pursue leadership roles or to speak up too much, especially in front of men.

It seemed as if sexual purity became the most important thing the youth group could teach us. Our purity seemed directly and exclusively linked to whether or not we had had sex. So once we were back in the real world, we constantly asked each other the most important question: How far is too far? The answer always seemed to elude us. We needed to know how far we could go in our sexual exploration while still being considered pure, because purity was the most important thing.

Part of the problem with the True Love Waits movement is that it wasn't incredibly effective. One study showed that while those who took a purity pledge were less likely to engage in sexual intercourse, it didn't seem to affect their other sexual behavior.[1] Another study, published in 2009, showed that 82 percent of those who made a pledge denied doing so five years later. Furthermore, their sexual behavior, including premarital sex and the incidence of sexually transmitted disease, was very similar to those who had never made a pledge.[2] Cool. So basically, all our generation got out of purity culture was the illusion of acting like we weren't having sex when we either were or were skirting the line. Either way, an abundance of problems and ignorance surrounded the issue of sex.

And then we got married. We wore pretty clothes, exchanged rings and vows, celebrated with a dance party, and then—*bam!*— we were supposed to flip a switch and instantly go from believing sex was bad and immoral to seeing it as not only good and acceptable, but as necessary. And we absolutely couldn't understand why that switch didn't flip the second we became a Mr. and a Mrs. Whether we waited or not, Christian youth were often shocked to find they didn't immediately have incredible sex the first night of their honeymoon.

If this is or was your experience, I want to be sure you know you're not alone. As the resident initiator of all sex conversations with my friends, I'm here to tell you that most Christian women I know struggle with sex in some form or fashion. For some it's a lack of desire. They simply don't really want to have sex with their husbands—likely because every message they were ever given about sex was negative. (If that describes you, however, that might also be a sign that you need to get your hormones checked because that makes a huge difference as well!) Other women struggle to enjoy sex because they don't really know what they're doing and don't know where to go to learn in a way that isn't saturated with worldly messages. In general, Christian women are struggling in their sex lives when we should be the ones having the best sex ever. Personally, I attribute that to what we've been taught.

From my own experience and my conversations with other women, I believe the overarching point most of us took away from our youth group discussions was that our bodies are bad. We got the message that we were solely responsible for the sexual purity of our brothers, and the sexual purity of our brothers (and ourselves) is the most important thing. Our churches likely didn't tell us this implicitly, but what else were we supposed to take away from being told repeatedly that our bodies made guys sin and therefore it was our job to hide them away? I remember being taught that men think about sex every seven seconds while women think about it approximately never. No wonder, then, that we expected our husbands to want to have sex all the time and we stuffed down our natural desires, assuming our sex drives should be nonexistent. All of these messed-up messages also meant young single women were unfamiliar with their own bodies and felt ashamed and dirty whenever they experienced any feelings of sexual desire. And if we did mess up and act on

those desires, we were instantly inun-
dated with shame and guilt. Either way,
the intimate act of sex that God called
good had been weaponized to encourage guilt and mistrust. We were eman-
cipated from our sexuality but didn't
know how to get it back.

> THE INTIMATE ACT OF SEX THAT
> GOD CALLED GOOD HAD BEEN
> WEAPONIZED TO ENCOURAGE
> GUILT AND MISTRUST. WE
> WERE EMANCIPATED FROM OUR
> SEXUALITY BUT DIDN'T KNOW
> HOW TO GET IT BACK.

The boys weren't given much either.
When I've talked with the men who grew
up in the purity culture generation, most explained they were simply
told not to do it and then sent out to play sports. Literally. Until I
began my research for this chapter, I was sure that was a fluke—surely
there was more to uncover to the conversation these boys had with
their leaders. But no, they were also not told how or why to abstain
from sex. As a result, I suspect that a lot of guys went about their
business anyway, with no tools to avoid temptation and little sense
they had any responsibility since that was all heaped on the girls.

Whether male or female, the lucky ones were simply steeped in
sexual ignorance. The unfortunate ones completely deconstructed
their faith and walked away from the church entirely. And I'll be
honest, I don't entirely blame them. The message of purity culture
exerted dominance over both men and women and had the power
of silence on its side.

BACK TO THE SOURCE

To some people, Christian culture seems so anti-sex you'd think it
wasn't originally created by the God we serve. Many of us who grew
up in the church during the nineties learned to categorize sex in the
column of "bad things," and I think that has a lot to do with why
not many married Christians are having great sex.

That makes me wonder: What if we just went back to what God says about sex? What if we stripped away the dos and don'ts, the implications and assumptions? What if we just went back to the Word?

News flash: God created sex. He created it for us to enjoy and take part in with our spouse, free of shame, allowing one to be wholly known by another. You literally can't make it two chapters into the Bible before you encounter God's design for our sexuality: "That is why a man leaves his father and mother and is united to his wife, and they become one flesh. Adam and his wife were both naked, and they felt no shame" (Genesis 2:24-25, NIV). Before the Fall, when sin infiltrated everything, sex was part of creation and it was *good*. Very good!

It was (and continues to be) a way for man and wife to connect, to form an intimate friendship, to become "one flesh." And if that term makes you feel a little weird, solidarity. But if you press into God's design for sex, you discover it's just one more way He gave us to fortify our marriages and to pursue physical, emotional, sexual, and spiritual unity.

I think the Father intended us to be sexual with one person because He knows (and invented) the inner workings of sex to create a bond between two people, making them one. When we engage in any kind of touch, sexual or not, our bodies release oxytocin—the hormone responsible for connection and bonding. And during orgasm, our bodies release dopamine, the "feel good" hormone, which also has bonding properties. In other words, our bodies were literally created to connect with another human via the act of sex. When we function outside of God's plan for sex, the natural consequences—painful breakups, unplanned pregnancies, sexually transmitted infections, etc.—lead to pain.

Still, I think the teachings of purity culture hurt God's heart.

First, while I believe God created us for sexual intimacy with only one individual, I'm also of the (sometimes unpopular) opinion that no sin (including of the sexual variety) is greater than the other, no matter how much the church attempts to create a hierarchy of which are better or worse. Second, I don't believe He intended for His kids to learn about His gift through the shaming and secrecy that too often is part of the purity culture. And I think we can do a far better job of educating ourselves about God's intentions for sex if we just go to the source. Just as with any other part of our lives and relationships, should we not be learning about it from Scripture? Because guess what? There's plenty of Scripture about sex and how it was intended to be used.

A quick flip through Song of Solomon and Proverbs will show you that Solomon, one of God's most beloved sons, was a big fan of sex. If sex is the dirty thing we've made it out to be, what do we make of verses like Proverbs 5:18-19: "Rejoice in the wife of your youth, a lovely deer, a graceful doe. Let her breasts fill you at all times with delight; be intoxicated always in her love" (ESV)? Why do we only know the verses like 1 Corinthians 6:18 ("Flee from sexual immorality. Every other sin a person commits is outside the body, but the sexually immoral person sins against his own body" ESV), but not the fun ones that tell us that sex is good and meant to be enjoyed? Song of Solomon has got to be purity culture's worst nightmare. Admittedly, Solomon didn't help his own cause; he wasn't exactly monogamous and suffered the consequences of functioning outside God's intention for marriage. But he also pulled no punches when it came to being honest about the beautiful nature and experience of sex within the confines God intended it.

Whether we're married and have been struggling with our sexual relationship for years, or we're single and unsure how to function healthily in this area of our lives, we can undo the messed-up messages we received and begin to walk in freedom with our Father's help. Because sex is good. And I don't mean in a good sex way. I mean that God created it and gave it to us and therefore it must be good, since the Father didn't make anything that wasn't good.

GOD CALLED IT GOOD

So how do we strip away the grime and allow sex to take its appropriate place in the list of good things God created? In my experience, that's something only you, your partner (if you have one), a good counselor, and God can do. The best thing my husband and I ever did was to just start talking, which was years into our marriage because even though we were husband and wife, it still felt taboo to discuss our mindset blocks or, heaven forbid, what we did and didn't like. We started by telling each other when we enjoyed things and when we didn't. Then we got comfortable enough to ask for things we liked, both during sex and in conversation outside of the bedroom (or kitchen or living room). Sure, it felt a little awkward at first, but we jokingly refer to our sex life as a video game, and I swear to you that when we started having open dialogue about sex, we unlocked a whole new level.

Talk to God about your sex life and sexuality, because I promise you He cares. There isn't a part of your life that God doesn't want to lead you toward freedom in, sex included. If He created it and designed it for your enjoyment, don't you think He wants to help you see it the way He intended? So ask Him to reveal His perfect plan for sexuality, to undo the muddied messages you've been taught, and to help you walk in sexual freedom that simultaneously honors His plan and shrugs off the excesses of purity culture.

Once you've discovered that sex is good and created by God, the next hurdle to cross is often to believe that sex can be fun and is meant to be enjoyed, not just tolerated. Popular culture doesn't help with this narrative, doubling down on the message women get from the church. Almost every sitcom or romantic comedy film has wives rolling their eyes and rolling over as their husbands paw at them in clumsy sexual advances. It can be difficult to untie yourself from unhealthy views on healthy sex when you're getting these weird messages from both the church and the world.

Women are told they aren't supposed to have a sex drive and men that they're supposed to want it all the time. But what if that's not the hand your partnership has been dealt? What if the woman has the higher drive? Or what if the man finds himself the one really wrestling with the lies of purity culture? Or what if both struggle to believe sex is good and meant to be enjoyed? Or what if you're not yet married and every hint of sexual desire brings another crushing load of guilt? If any of those scenarios describe you, I encourage you to turn to Scripture. Take a spin through Proverbs and Song of Solomon and hear the ways King Solomon waxed poetic about the beautiful nature of sex. If you're not yet married, let his words encourage you and do the work of undoing the damaging directives purity culture and the secular world gave you. And if you're married, verses like Proverbs 5:18-19 should serve as permission to start figuring out what enjoying your married sex life looks like.

As Christians we are called to look different from the world. Paul was super clear about this when he said, "Do not be conformed to this world, but be transformed by the renewal of your mind" (Romans 12:2, ESV). Why should sexuality and our sex lives be any different? As children of the One who created sex (and all the other good things), should we not be the ones with the most healthy sexuality? Should we not reject both the world's empty promises around sexuality along with any vestiges of shame we may have picked up from purity culture? The sex lives of married couples should model for others how to fully give ourselves to and communicate with each other as we enjoy sex the way God intended. Yes, we preserve sex for marriage, but we also know that our purity and value as humans aren't tied to whom we've slept with but are defined by the finished work of the Cross.

We give our kids a better understanding of why sex belongs inside marriage by telling them that it is good and important and explaining why God designed it to be between a husband and wife. Our college students should know why they're not engaging in hot and heavy hookups like all their friends—and not just because they were shamed into abstinence.

The collateral damage from the purity culture and True Love Waits is on display. I believe one reason Christian divorce rates rival those of non-Christians is because our ideas about sex are so warped and unbiblical. But if you don't think God is bigger than some books and a conference, I have news for you. He is. And just because you may have walked out of that era with a bit of a limp and some lies to undo, the truth is that God will help you do it. He wants to do it. He wants His children to experience the full goodness of the gift of sex. The manual to undoing the mixed messages you received is right in the Good Book: "He redeems your life from the Pit; he crowns you with faithful love and compassion" (Psalm 103:4). No matter how deep you think you've fallen, God not only will lovingly rescue you, He longs to restore you.

Chapter 13

WHY DO FRIENDSHIP BREAKUPS HURT SO MUCH?

One of Satan's cleverest attacks is getting us to pour our time
and energy into people who resent the grace we share and
who will never change, keeping us from spending time with
and focusing on others whom we can love and serve.

GARY THOMAS, *WHEN TO WALK AWAY*

BEFORE WE GO FURTHER, can we all agree that friendship breakups are approximately a hundred times worse than dating breakups? I've been through my fair share of both, and I'll take ending a relationship with some dumb boy over losing my best friend any day. (I'm not talking about divorce here, by the way.)

As women, we just bond with one another differently—more deeply and personally—than men tend to connect with each other. We become engrained in one another's lives. I often use the analogy of a knitted sweater to describe the relationship between girlfriends: It's difficult to tell where one strand begins and another ends. And as anyone who has ever worn a knitted sweater will tell you, if one string gets snagged, the whole thing starts to unravel.

So it is with the ending of friendship. It often feels as though you've lost a piece of yourself, doesn't it? Not only is there now this gaping chasm in your life, but she took a bit of you with her when she left. Sometimes a friend will leave willingly for reasons that are assuredly reasonable to them, and that may, in fact, be reasonable. Other times you feel forced to distance yourself from a friend for reasons of your own. And sometimes the two of you simply drift apart, the currents of distance, busy calendars, children, and differing opinions pulling you in different directions until you look up and realize how far apart you are. That's really the most idyllic ending of a friendship—the subtle moving apart of lives, threads cleanly pulling themselves free of one another, no snags, no tears, just the ending of a season marked by a grateful heart for the times you shared.

But that's not really what we're referring to when talking about friendship breakups. We mean the violent ripping apart of lives embedded within each other, screaming wounds of betrayal and hurt, the uncomfortable and painful process of untangling and frogging (knitting slang for undoing all your hard work; "rip it, rip it"—get it?), all of which brings its own heartache and trauma. Sometimes it's the friend who really knows you—the deep, intimate parts of you—who essentially takes a pair of scissors to the thread that held you together, saying, "I no longer want this." Or maybe you're the one holding the shears, wearing enough pain and hurt that you consider ruining the sweater.

I wish I could tell you I have minimal experience with these situations and the resulting barrage of emotions, but unfortunately, I'm a bit of a veteran when it comes to the excruciating process of friendships ending. Some of them were undisputedly my fault, especially during my hustling days when I was getting after it and chasing down fame to the extent that I didn't notice I was simultaneously becoming an astonishingly craptastic friend. If it didn't "serve" me, I didn't have time for it, friendship included. I don't want to make it sound like I was some kind of monster—I don't think I was—but I definitely wasn't a great friend. Because being a good friend wasn't a priority, I would do things like forget about plans or ignore someone who needed a shoulder to cry on in lieu of tackling my to-do list.

Once I emerged from hustle culture, I learned a lot about myself, about what real, biblical friendship looks like, and the many ways in which I needed to grow to look like the kind of friend God calls us to be.

I resonate with the way pastor and author Dharius Daniels puts it in his sermon "Who's at Your Table?":

> Everybody should be loved biblically, valued equally, but treated differently. Just because everyone is of equal value doesn't mean they add equal value to you. And it's our responsibility to make sure the people who mean the most to us don't get the least of us.[1]

I went on an apology tour, intentionally sitting down with women whom I love and value so I could look them in the eyes while expressing my sorrow for casting them aside in my own stupid pursuit of something that I thought would fulfill me.

The first stop on my tour was my own kitchen table. I sat across from a friend who had been with me since our babies were born. I confessed that the people I loved the most (including her) had gotten the least of me during the last few years, and that those days were over. I was done being distracted and self-serving, and I promised to be the kind of friend I had been early on. There were tears and the brutal honesty that years of friendship make space for. I was so grateful when she accepted my apology, and we've remained good friends since. Our lives began to be knit together again, even as I continued on my apology tour. Over time, the girls' nights recommenced, the text threads fired back up, our kids were overjoyed to be seeing one another consistently again, and life felt full.

Yet not all the stops on my tour were so successful. My apologies weren't enough for a few of my former friends. Honestly, I was experiencing the natural consequence of choosing myself over God and others. It never feels great to have apologies rejected and attempts to reconnect turned down, but I had to remind myself that the choice was theirs to make, not mine. All I could do was own the ways I had contributed to the unraveling. I knew that God's intention when we confess our sin and forgive others isn't to stay defeated. So even though some people on my apology tour couldn't see the difference in me, I recognized that didn't mean the change didn't exist, and I had to be okay with that.

The Lord used my newfound desire to glorify Him instead of myself to grow me in a multitude of ways, one of them being in friendship. I wanted to become a better friend, but I had been clueless that Scripture is busting at the seams with directions on how to show up for your people. I didn't know it contained clear guidance for navigating difficult seasons with a friend, like Colossians 3:13 ("Bear with each other and forgive one another if any of you has a grievance against someone. Forgive as the Lord forgave you" (NIV). It had never occurred to me that John 15:12 could be viewed in the context of friendship, used as guidance for love between friends ("My command is this: Love each other as I have loved you" (NIV).

Now I started digging into the Word instead of self-help books. I began applying those principles to my life and watched in wonder as my friendships thrived. I realized then that I have not always followed Paul's instruction to allow others to carry my burdens or to carry burdens for others (see Galatians 6:2). Maybe if we spent more time looking for the friends whose shoulders are sagging under the weight of life and walked arm in arm with them, our own lives would feel a little less heavy.

And just as I was learning how to be a better friend, the Crappy Christian Co. was born. After years of asking God to point me in the right direction when it came to using the gifts He'd given me, I had gotten the green light from Him to start a podcast. I had asked and asked and continually heard *not yet*—not no, more along the lines of "you're barely keeping your head above water with what you have on your plate, girlfriend." And as time passed and my capacity to juggle the things life threw at me matured, it finally felt like He was saying *okay, now—go!* And completely unexpectedly, that podcast took off at lightning speed, garnering listens and follows faster than I could keep up with. It was like once I had let go of what I thought success and fulfillment would look like and submitted to God and His definitions, He told me, "Buckle up, let's go." The months that followed were wild, in the best way—I felt as if I were drinking out of a fire hydrant of blessings and goodness. I finally had my feet planted firmly on the path God wanted me on, and I was running at full pace, arm in arm with Him, beside myself with excitement over what He was doing and where we were going. But there were people in my life who didn't share in that excitement. That's when I learned to navigate a different sort of friendship breakup.

The common narrative tells us to expect to lose friends when the going gets tough. In his song "Find Out Who Your Friends Are," the great philosopher (and country music singer) Tracy Lawrence reflects that everyone seems to want to be close to us when we're at the pinnacle of success. But he adds, "Let one of those rocks give way, then you slide back down, look up and see who's around then."[2] The experience of having people walk away from you when you're down sucks. The hands you expected to be extended to help you just aren't there, and you're left to wonder whether you even mattered to those friends at all.

Have you ever lost a friend because of your achievements? That is a whole different ball game, friends. When the people you expect to go with you as your trajectory aims upwards, the friends you thought would be cheering you every time you experienced a win, just disappear—that hits you differently. (A necessary caveat: If you've had some success and thus turned into a jerk of Kanye West circa 2009 proportions, you're probably going to lose friends, and you might even deserve to. The worst thing we can do as believers and as friends is let our success go to our heads and turn us into different people. Like me, you've probably watched this unfold over and over in the social media age, and the fall from the top is a long one. So don't even set yourself up for that failure. Instead, sit down, be humble, and love the people God puts around you well.)

I'm just going to come out and say it: I've lost friends because of my success. And it's the worst. I've walked with friends as they lost friends due to their success, and that's the worst too. Your "success" doesn't have to look like mine or anyone else's for it to impact your relationships. Your achievements may stack up in the corporate world or in your marriage, they may be financial or material or succeeding at being a really great mom. It could be as simple as stepping into something that another person wanted, even if you weren't aware of it. Jealousy and competition are like termites eating at the foundation of relationships, and half the time you don't even know they're there until the house is crumbling. Envy isn't a new phenomenon, and its impact on friendships has existed since the beginning. Don't believe me?

When David came to Saul and entered his service, Saul loved him very much, and David became his armor-bearer. Then Saul sent word to Jesse: "Let David remain in my service, for he has found favor with me."

1 SAMUEL 16:21-22

David lived around 1,000 BC, so a really long time ago. (Like I said, tension around success has existed since the beginning.) At the urging of one of his servants, the king of Israel at the time, Saul, employed David into his service. Known as a talented musician, David played the lyre to help Saul chill out, and he also served as Saul's armor-bearer. The king quickly became a big fan of the former shepherd boy. Then something changed. In my Bible, just two chapters apart, are the subheadings "David in Saul's Court" and "Saul Attempts to Kill David." Um, hello plot twist. You see, what happened between chapter 16 and chapter 18 was David's encounter with Goliath. Potentially the most massive success of David's lifetime was when he conquered the Philistine soldier with five stones and a sling, an undertaking not even the fiercest Israelite soldier had been willing to take on. Saul then sent David out on other military missions, and David's achievements piled up until the streets were filled with people singing his praises.

Saul's response to David's newfound fame was to hurl a spear at his head. Now look, I hope you haven't experienced this too. If you have, please let me know; I feel like it would be a great story. But have you ever had someone fling verbal spears at you?

Oh, I see you got yourself a little job.
What makes you think you can do what you're doing?
So, you think you're a writer now.

The fact is, people don't have to put hands on you to hurt you. And often, it's those closest to us who react most negatively to our prosperity or even just our attempts to try something new. I'll never forget the time a friend looked me dead in the face and said, "I just don't understand why I have to watch you live out your dreams while mine sit on the sideline." I was completely unprepared to navigate this new reality in which the people I expected to at minimum be excited for me were, in fact, trying to tear me down.

Or when a yearslong friendship ended because even though my friend and I had started out doing the same thing at the same pace, my pace had quickened while hers hadn't. And it didn't matter how much I tried to take her with me on this adventure, my success had choked our relationship of the life it once held.

When hurtful comments keep coming like spears aimed at our heads, we often keep handing those weapons back because we love these people and share a history. We dodge the blows as best we can, maybe even take a few steps in a different direction, but at the end of the day we end up taking the collateral damage of their own baggage, insecurity, and pain. Saul's heart turning from love to hate for David was a Saul problem, not a "David + his success" issue.

The regrettable truth is that you can't always take people with you. No matter how much you want to. No matter how much work you've done to better yourself, how much you show up, how much you lean in—there are people who just aren't meant to come with you. This doesn't mean people and relationships are disposable. Scripture gives a lot of instruction on how to love others and walk through difficult times (see Luke 6:27; Romans 12:9; Matthew 18:15).

But along the way we've twisted the Bible to mean we're supposed to take a beating, and I'm just not here for that. When we are blessed in a way a friend wants to be (or vice versa), God desires for us to lean in and extend love to each other, even though our circumstances are different. Maybe you got pregnant and someone you love struggles with infertility. Perhaps a friend has earned her degree and you desperately wish you could go back to college and finish your own. Maybe your financial situation has changed, which makes people who know your economic history uncomfortable or envious. Perhaps they have seen money change certain individuals (which it absolutely can) and assume it will do the same to you. So they don't even give you the benefit of the doubt and begin to back away. It may be that your situation is similar to mine—a windfall of sorts happens and when you turn to celebrate with the ones you love, you're met with disdain and resentment instead of excitement. Sometimes people's pain becomes so great they simply cannot stand to be near a person who doesn't feel the same hurt—or their pain causes them to lash out.

THE BEAUTY OF BOUNDARIES

Though the word is tossed around a lot, I don't think Christians really understand the concept of boundaries—the reality that you can love someone deeply and value them in the way God intends but still say "this far and no further." That's sometimes the deepest expression of love we can give someone who continues to hurt us. Often boundaries are treated as harsh or unloving in the Christian community, as if we've forgotten that Jesus Himself often exemplified the importance of boundaries throughout His earthly ministry. Like when He walked away from a crowd that wanted to hurt Him (see Luke 4:29-30), or when He challenged the religious leaders who asked Him baiting questions (see Matthew 21–22).

> YOU CAN LOVE SOMEONE DEEPLY AND VALUE THEM IN THE WAY GOD INTENDS BUT STILL SAY "THIS FAR AND NO FURTHER."

If Jesus had boundaries, do you not think He wants us to have them too? Reminder: There's a difference between walls and boundaries. Walls are often built as a response to wounds and badly handled relationships. They're intended to keep closeness at bay and people as far from truly knowing you as possible. But boundaries? Boundaries usher people into appropriate relationships, remind them what is permissible, and make it possible to function healthily with others. If you live through the difficult ending of close relationships, you learn the importance of boundaries. That sometimes a friend like Saul turns into an enemy like Saul. Cutting off those friendships can feel like we're killing a part of ourselves (and maybe we are), but I've learned from experience that sometimes God removes what we won't because He knows we can no longer thrive and flourish under the weight of it.

Because while you're trying desperately to hold on to someone, God hears things you don't and knows things you don't. While you're trying to hike a person onto your back so they can take this mountain with you, the Father is asking you to put that person down and continue on with Him. This is the part of friendship and friendship breakups that doesn't get talked about.

I believe the Father's heart is for reconciliation and redemption. His ultimate hope for our relationships is that they mend and in mending they grow stronger. But the reality is that we live on a broken earth and do life with other flawed humans, and often it doesn't go the way of God's design. We need God's truth to remind us that it's okay to set boundaries or to walk away from toxic people, though it's important to seek His guidance in the midst of all of it. So instead of pretending like friendship breakups don't happen or acting like their impact isn't deep and wide, I want you to know that, if you've experienced this, you're not alone. And I want you to get back on the road of serving and loving people who don't want to take you down.

When David faced the betrayal of Saul, he could have responded by giving up on relationships entirely. Instead, David went on to have deep, meaningful friendships with Saul's son Jonathan and the prophet Nathan—friendships that exemplify the biblical standard for healthy relationships. David did this by keeping his focus on his covenant with God. You can do the same. You don't have to be derailed by relationship strife. That's not to say it won't hurt like crazy (because it likely will) or that you won't have healing to do (because you definitely will), but friendship breakups don't have to take you out of the game.

Still, losing a close friendship can feel like losing a limb. After all, such friends are so deeply ingrained in every part of our lives that when those relationships unravel, it truly is like the knitted-sweater fabric of life unraveling around us. Grief comes in waves, and you feel all alone in your heartache. Well, solidarity, sister. You're not the first and you won't be the last to be flat on your back in the wake of losing someone you thought you'd grow old and gray alongside.

THE PAYOFF OF PRUNING

Have you ever seen a grapevine being pruned? Personally, I always assumed it to be a delicate procedure: a snip here, a snip there, gentle hands navigating the intricacies of the leaves and fruit for fear of harming it. In actuality, pruning is kind of violent. It involves hacking and sawing, tearing away old, dead branches. The person wielding the shears leans against the vine, putting bodily effort behind snapping off pieces. To the untrained eye, pruning can look a lot like killing. But if you don't cut away all the dead junk, the dead junk is what will actually kill a plant. And so it is with our lives, specifically the relationships we would have preferred to keep that God intentionally removes. Often, we don't know we're being pruned as it's happening because we're so sure God is, in fact, killing us. But I promise, He's not.

You may never get to understand why, but you can hold tight to the truth that He uses what the enemy means for harm for our good. Sometimes God has to clear distractions out so you can focus on Him better. Sometimes He wants to remove something we think is good for us but just . . . isn't. But everything that happens in this life works together for the good of those who serve Him, even the hard things (see Romans 8:28).

So whether you are mourning a relationship loss that is due to your success, the low points in life, or your own awful behavior (all of which I've experienced, by the way), it does get better. I promise. You will start to walk with less of a limp, propped up by Jesus, who never leaves your side. You will start to trust again, let people in again, laugh and enjoy another person's company again. I want you to know that not every ended relationship comes back together, even if that's what you want. Sometimes God removes people from your life permanently. But every once in a while, after a time of grief and forgiveness, your phone will light up with a text from someone you thought you'd never hear from again. And that message may contain the apology you never thought would come, the olive branch you never thought would be extended. Maybe you, like me, will be forced to fight back tears in a crowded coffee shop as a friend who is engrained in every memory you've ever had, the friend you'd lost, makes her way back into your life, with humility and kindness and understanding. Because God can do that. God can put back together things you never thought you'd get to see be whole again.

You will heal, and sometimes you will even be able to knit that old comfortable sweater back together again, the threads put back into place, albeit often a little more ragged than before. But it's a sweater worth wearing, just like you're a human worth loving.

Chapter 14

SHOULD I JUST FAKE FORGIVENESS?

When we forgive, we set a prisoner free
and then discover the prisoner was us.

LEWIS B. SMEDES

IT TOOK ME YEARS OF WRESTLING with Scripture's instruction for believers to forgive as Christ has forgiven us to understand the biblical principle of forgiveness—a lifetime of desiring the freedom and goodness I knew would come with Christlike forgiveness but struggling to get there. And like everyone else living in a broken world, I was constantly presented with opportunities for practice. Familial wounds piled on top of friendship hurts compounded by romantic pain meant there was a mountain of people I needed to forgive. Now, retrospectively, I can see why I didn't grasp biblical forgiveness. It wasn't because I didn't understand it: Thanks to the Bible, I had the blueprint right in front of me. It was because I didn't like the concept.

I was stuck between the rock and hard place of not wanting to give people a "pass" and say what they had done was okay while also wanting to look like Jesus. A bit of an oxymoron, yes, but I never said it made sense. What it did do was cause an epic, yearslong internal war. I'm not naturally inclined to be the most trusting individual, but ever since handing my life over to Jesus I have grown to have a deep and consuming desire to look like Him in life and mind. So here I was with a very warped definition of forgiveness that in fact made forgiveness impossible. I had created what I now call "fake forgiveness." Fake forgiveness looks pretty on the outside. It looks like extending an unwarranted olive branch, refusing to engage in negative talk about the person who hurt you, and sometimes even apologizing for things you really have no right to be sorry for. Fake forgiveness goes above and beyond to take the high road and attempts to keep the peace rather than make it.

But fake forgiveness is a cancer.

While you do all the right things externally and wax poetic about extending forgiveness, nothing has changed on the inside. You lie awake at night replaying everything that happened, overanalyzing and reexperiencing the pain someone caused. You stalk that person's Instagram to see if they've said anything that could even remotely be taken to be "about" you, as if you're seeking out more ways to be hurt by them. You constantly talk about how wounded you are by the other party to those closest to you in the name of processing, but really, it's become a compulsion. You slowly but surely are eaten alive by your hurt, which is metastasizing into bitterness, anger, and can even turn into obsession.

Like the time I fake forgave my college boyfriend for cheating on me and then stayed with him. We'd been together for years, toxic as our relationship was, and we were determined to stick it out. Neither of us was even a shade of our healthiest selves—the preened and pretty versions of us showed up to church and college ministry together, but behind the scenes it was ugly. Unchecked and unapologetic sin ran rampant through our relationship, and because of that, we fought. A lot. We fought and we sinned and we brought out the worst in each other, but I do think we loved one another. As the final days of our relationship began to loom, we took a "break." We hadn't broken up, but we had agreed to take a breather from the toxic sludge of a relationship we were both drowning in.

Then one day he called me, which was against the rules. But I loved him, so I answered. My normally boisterous and loud boyfriend faintly whispered a request for me to come to his house. Sure something was wrong, I sped over and knocked on his door, expecting blood. But what I found was . . . sorrow. He had betrayed me with another girl. He didn't know how it had happened, he said, but it didn't mean anything—it was just a mistake. The boy got down on his knees and apologized while my heart broke into a million pieces.

I had laid so many of my dreams aside for him, and we were so entangled in each other's lives that I honestly couldn't see a way out. So I stayed, even after this ultimate betrayal. Sadly, history repeated itself not long after our break ended, when another girl made her way between us. Thankfully, miraculously by then I really was done. When I found out about the next girl, I simply looked him in the eyes, said "okay" and walked out. And I never looked back. I was so damaged by this version of love that this new betrayal didn't even hurt. It had become par for the course.

Fake forgiveness was part of how I had gotten there. I loved him, so each time he hurt me, I took him back with open arms, generally acting like everything was fine. I never threw his messups in his face, never held them over his head. We carried on our attractive facade of two people in a long-term relationship who loved Jesus and went to church every Sunday. But, alone at night, I often struggled to fall asleep. I lost lots of weight because I was so tied up in knots. My fake forgiveness metastasized into constant knock-down, drag-out fights, borderline emotional abuse, and the most toxic relationship I've ever been in.

Worst of all, I had established no boundaries in our relationship, no consequences for his poor behavior, so I had nothing to protect myself from the emotional blowback whenever anything went sideways. Because I had never dealt with the emotional pain caused by several betrayals and, worse, had acted like everything was fine for so long, everyone around me assumed our final breakup would be no different. That I would be fine. But the cancer of fake forgiveness had become too much, and the pain burst out of me and over everyone around me. I was a disaster of Chernobyl proportions.

I'm not saying I ended up bitter solely due to my lack of limits and attempts at fake forgiveness. That boy was absolutely responsible for breaking my heart and making bad choices. But for the years right after that, all I could see was how awful he had been and how much he had hurt me. I knew I was still refusing to genuinely forgive him, content and comfortable in my anger because it meant what he had done was wrong.

I wish I could say that experience snapped me out of my reliance on fake forgiveness, but it didn't. For the next ten years I continued the practice with other friends, extending perfectly pruned olive branches to them while acting out the Battle of Stirling Bridge from *Braveheart* on the inside (minus the epic inspirational speech via Mel Gibson). I was a woman at war with her pain and hurt, unsure of what to do with it or where to put it, so I just shoved it off into the dark corners. I had years of biblical knowledge about forgiveness stored up in my brain, but I couldn't get them to make the trek to my heart. I knew our call was to forgive the unforgivable because that was what Jesus had done. I'm still not completely sure why I held on to this faux version of forgiveness for so long, but it probably had to do with the hall-pass nature of what forgiveness can feel like: If we extend real, unbridled, unearned forgiveness to someone, aren't we also giving the person a get-out-of-jail-free card for what they've done? I didn't yet understand that forgiveness is for both parties. That it sets both of you free. I still thought it was all for the offender and a simple brush-off for the offended.

STOPPING THE BLEEDING

It would take another great betrayal for me to finally wrap my thick skull around what Scripture is talking about when it instructs us to forgive others' trespasses. It took losing two best friends, watching those ex–best friends becoming friends themselves, and that drama driving me absolutely insane for me to finally get it.

I am blessed to have many wise, deeply rooted in Christ, incredible women of God in my life. Women who challenge me and pull me up, who love me as I am but refuse to let me stay in my sin. The ones who will ask the hard, uncomfortable questions and will tell me the truth, even if it stings a little bit. As a result, during the last few years I have pruned and thinned out my relationships. But the great thing about clearing things out is that you're able to see what you have even more distinctly. Kind of like when you tell your kids you're about to throw away the toys they don't play with and they suddenly realize that they have some really great, quality toys, which they start playing with all the time.

In just eight months, I had lost two friendships that I'd thought would span a lifetime, and it was messy and hard. One thing that made all of it even more difficult was that I couldn't let go. Or I should say, I wouldn't. So when two people who were strangers to one another, that I had intimately done life with, somehow found friendship with each other online, it wrecked shop in my life. Because I hadn't forgiven them individually, this new pain was the final chink in the already unsteady dam holding things back. I walked with a limp; my wounds so compounded I was just bleeding out on the people around me. But never fear! I still looked like I had it together on the outside. But the people God had pulled tight around me were absolutely not getting the best of me. They were getting a sad version of love that had been depleted and crippled. Using the word *obsessed* here stings, but because I didn't know how to let go, I became obsessed with the pain and betrayal. It infiltrated almost every moment, bringing with it that stomach-lurching sense of anxiety, keeping everything that had been said and done near the surface.

I wasn't a saint in the scenario, but because losing the two of them had been so hard, watching their new friendship blossom felt like too much. I talked about it constantly, seeking both confirmation that what was happening was wrong and also hoping someone would magically be able to fix it all. I was so hyperfocused on what had been done to me that I didn't know how to take my eyes off my own pain and love the ones who had stayed with me. I cried at random, engulfed in the cocktail of betrayal and misery I couldn't seem to put down. This went on for months—months I drowned myself in pain, resentment, and preoccupation. To date my husband says it's one of the few situations he's ever seen truly knock me flat on my back.

One of the friends God gave me in that season is also the most incredible wordsmith you've ever met in your life. Her way with words never ceases to both amaze and level me as they shoot directly into my heart, making me feel seen and heard and known. One day in the midst of the limping and bleeding and my saying what I'd been saying for months, she said, "I don't think you've yet acknowledged what happened and therefore have been unable to forgive and to shed the pain and the weight."

Insert record screeching sound here

Three words jumped out of her sentence and punched me in the face—*Acknowledge. Forgive. Shed.* Honestly, I don't think I fully comprehended right then what she had told me (and definitely not the impact it would have on my life moving forward). I just knew that my soul needed those words. They were a balm for a heart that was screaming out in pain and hurt but couldn't figure out how to heal. Now, I'm a sucker for a good process. Give me steps to follow and I'm ready to crush whatever you've set before me. And I'm a firm believer that God uses other people in our lives to communicate His truth in exactly the way we need it. I needed steps and now I had them; all I had to do was turn to Scripture to unpack what they meant and move forward. Her words served as a spark that simultaneously burned down my presupposed version of forgiveness while giving me light to see the gift God actually offers to us when we forgive. I guess I had already felt like I was on fire for months, but this was different. This was a purposeful blaze, destroying what needed to go and lighting up the truth.

And, boy, was I in for a ride as I took those three words to heart.

ACKNOWLEDGE

Come to me, all who labor and are heavy laden, and I will
give you rest. Take my yoke upon you, and learn from me,
for I am gentle and lowly in heart, and you will find rest
for your souls. For my yoke is easy, and my burden is light.
MATTHEW 11:28-30, ESV

I'm a mover. A shaker. My husband likens me to a shark because he's convinced if I stop moving and doing, I'll die. For a lot of my life, *rest* was a four-letter word both in thought and theory. So when I started digging into the three words my friend had given me and found these verses in Matthew, I was kind of like, *Really, God? We're going to talk about rest when it comes to forgiveness?* I slowly realized that while the entire text is obviously important, the words I needed were *heavy laden*. I won't bore you with the Greek word used there, but I will tell you its full translation is "overload . . . causing someone to be (literally) '*weighted*-down.'"[1] And there I was, feeling like I was carrying a four-ton mass made up of grief, pain, and wounds. I was both literally and metaphorically weighed down, not only trying to shoulder a boulder but also constantly looking backward because I wouldn't forgive. And here was my sweet Father asking me to put down that burden. To let Him have it and to rest. Not because what others had done was okay, not because I was magically over it, but because He is the provider of rest for our souls that surpasses all understanding. Not only is He the provider, He's the doer, because the truth is sometimes we just don't have what it takes to forgive. Sometimes the hurt is too deep, the pain too strong, and so we just end up holding on to it because we can't let go of it on our own, and we're unwilling to believe that God cares enough or is capable to do it for us, through us, with us. That's where I landed. Unable to do it on my own, knowing I needed Him to shoulder this pain as well as indwell in me the power to forgive so that I could live in freedom.

So I took a deep breath, and with tears running down my face, I wrote out all the hurtful things that had transpired in this specific situation from the really big to the seemingly insignificant. There were no qualifiers. If it had inflicted pain, it made it on the paper. I acknowledged my bruised and battered spirit, every stinging word, every pointed Instagram post, every hint of rejection and abandonment. I looked at my words and took them in, finally seeing my emotions for what they were rather than trying to hurry them to the closet where I thought they belonged. And then I looked my pain in the face and said, *I see you fully and completely, but I cannot carry you anymore.* In this exercise what I discovered was that I couldn't forgive what I hadn't looked at and seen in its fullness. I couldn't loosen my grip on pain if I wouldn't even look at its root. Acknowledging what had happened allowed me to see my hurt and no longer want to hold it inside.

Now typically this is where a Christian author would remind you that you also are a flawed human, often in need of forgiveness (which you are). But one thing I've found in doing life with others is that in some instances you and I are completely, unequivocally the ones who have been offended—situations in which we actually didn't do anything wrong and yet the church tells us it's got to somehow be a little bit our fault. And I just don't think that rhetoric is helpful in the healing and forgiving process. In fact, it may even cause us to hold our pain a little closer in an effort to feel its veracity. The truth is that sometimes people let us down. Part of acknowledging hurt is recognizing that we do not need to carry the guilt and shame that bubbled up when we were wounded.

We were not created to live our lives either consumed by our pain or pretending it doesn't exist. When Jesus talks about His yoke being easy and His burden being light, He means He is beside you in the yoke. It's not because everything is going to be hunky-dory; it's because even when the hard stuff comes, you will be shoulder to shoulder with the Creator of the universe. But if you refuse to acknowledge when things have gotten tough, you're also likely doing your best to stay out of the yoke.

> WE WERE NOT CREATED TO LIVE OUR LIVES EITHER CONSUMED BY OUR PAIN OR PRETENDING IT DOESN'T EXIST.

FORGIVE

> Let all bitterness and wrath and anger and clamor and
> slander be put away from you, along with all malice.
> Be kind to one another, tenderhearted, forgiving one
> another, as God in Christ forgave you.
>
> EPHESIANS 4:31-32, ESV

If these three words—*acknowledge, forgive,* and *shed*—were a mountain, forgiveness was the super challenging peak right before the top. Acknowledging hurt is a slow and steady ascent that can feel arduous. Actually forgiving the person who inflicted the pain often requires ropes and pulleys and a really great support system. That's because it demands the putting aside of yourself.

Forgiveness does not follow an apology. It does not wait for changed behavior. It is not predicated on justice being served, and it does not wait for you to feel ready. It is love in action the way Christ loved you. It is compelled by tenderheartedness, which the world makes us feel is a flaw but is in fact one of our greatest strengths. At the end of the day, we as believers are capable of forgiveness because of the finished work of the Cross—full stop. I can confidently tell you I would never, ever be able to forgive someone who has hurt me if I wasn't doing it in the shadow of Calvary. Knowing that Jesus chose forgiveness, even as He experienced the most excruciating death possible, compels and equips me to wipe the slate clean for people in my life. It may sound oversimplified, but there's just no other way. In fact, I think the reason many believers struggle with true forgiveness is because we don't live our lives in constant awe of the Cross. So when my ex–best friends became friends, I had a choice. I could keep a running list of all the ways they'd hurt me—maybe even make up ways to be offended—or I could look at the Cross, knowing that Jesus' blood covers the hurt the same way it covers my sins, and that that's enough. There's no need to get even or pursue my own justice. The Cross is enough.

Because here's the deal—in these verses, Paul very clearly lays out what happens if you and I don't forgive, and it's not pretty. I don't know about you, but I'd rather not be described as bitter, wrathful, angry, clamorous (what a great word), slanderous, or malicious. But I can tell you from experience that holding hurt and pain in your heart can do nothing but turn you into those things, and that's not how the Father intends His kids to walk through the hard parts of life. You have been given everything you need to forgive those who wrong you; the sacrifice has been made and the future justice promised. Now you need to choose to live like who you are and forgive, whether or not the one who wronged you is sorry.

SHED

Since we are surrounded by such a great cloud of witnesses, let us throw off everything that hinders and the sin that so easily entangles. And let us run with perseverance the race marked out for us, fixing our eyes on Jesus, the pioneer and perfecter of faith.

HEBREWS 12:1-2, NIV

Spoiler alert: We're at the best part. This is the part of the process where you hit the summit. Where you stop walking with a limp. Where you stop bleeding out. Where you start running again, even if you were sure you never would. Because let's be honest, not forgiving that old wound was holding you back. Carrying the burden of pain caused by others was entangling you and you weren't living in abundance. And here in Hebrews, the author tells you to throw that stuff off.

I'm a big believer that if Satan can't disable you, he'll distract you. And holding on to old hurts is *distracting*. When I was in my season of immense pain over those lost friendships, barely keeping my head above the emotional waters, the pain was truly all I could think and even talk about. I was so preoccupied and handicapped by my hurt that I had stopped running my race. I had taken my eyes off Jesus and set them on my loss, which I'm sure the enemy loved. Once I acknowledged and laid down my burdens and then forgave the people who had caused them (which was a monthslong process, by the way), shedding felt natural—though I wouldn't say easy.

I didn't need to drag my pain and resentment behind me anymore. I didn't need to pick at the scabs because I knew the Father wanted healing for me. Shedding meant letting go and moving forward. Shedding meant choosing to put it all down at the foot of the cross and never pick it up again. Shedding was different from forgiveness; the emotions and tangled-up feelings were gone. I had made a decisive turn. I no longer needed to know what these women were saying or doing because that no longer held power in my life. I was too busy to look anyway. Whenever I was tempted to look back at the people I'd lost, I began repeating these words to myself: *I release you, and in so doing, I release myself from giving you the power to hurt me again.* And by doing that, I experienced the beautiful release of feeling as free as Jesus had already made me. As I did, the bitterness began to slide away. I was noticeably less angry and jaded. Peace began to reign in my life again, both internally and externally. I had finally extended true forgiveness.

None of the people who hurt me so deeply have ever apologized. And you know what? That is okay. Because my forgiveness didn't come with terms and conditions. I forgave them because compared to the mountain of sin for which Jesus has forgiven me, the ways they hurt me are like a molehill. And I forgave them because I woke up and realized it was time to throw aside the things that were hindering me and get back to running my race.

Too often we talk about forgiveness as if it were a Band-Aid. Like a quick, get-over-it fix we apply to stop the bleeding and move on. But forgiveness isn't a pass for bad behavior. It doesn't mean you forget what's happened or move forward as if nothing ever did. Forgiveness is the act of extending the unearned grace you received to your fellow flawed humans. It's not exclusively for you or for them, but for both of you—an expression of what Christ did on the Cross, releasing each of you from the bonds and chaos of bitterness and tension. Forgiveness is rarely easy, but it is more bearable when you're in the yoke with Jesus and He's bearing some of the brunt with you.

But above all else, forgiveness is vital. The longer you refuse to forgive, the longer the torment will build in your body, heart, and mind. The longer you hold out on extending what cannot be earned, the more work it will take to untangle yourself from pain's tentacles. The sacrifice made on the cross thousands of years ago set you free in a myriad of ways—free from sin, free from shame, free from an eternity separated from the Father. It also gave you the power and freedom to forgive, fully and unconditionally, because that's what the Lord did for you and me.

That freedom isn't fake, but it is final.

Chapter 15

WHY DOES THE GOSPEL
MAKE ME UNCOMFORTABLE?

We seem to prefer the comfortable lie to the uncomfortable truth.
And we punish those who point out reality while rewarding those
who provide us with the comfort of illusion.

BILL MOYERS

I LEARNED MY ABCS BY MEMORIZING corresponding Bible verses in kindergarten at a private Christian school. By first grade we were doing Bible drills—those ultracompetitive games in which a teacher rattles off a Bible reference and the whole class frantically flips through their Bibles to get there as quickly as possible. Our spelling bees featured words from the Bible, and as I recall, teachers even found ways to incorporate Scripture in our math lessons, like using 1 Corinthians 14:33 ("God is not a God of disorder but of peace") to exemplify the beauty and structure of the way you can multiply by nines on your fingers (e.g., 9 x 2 = 18; if you hold down your second finger, you have a finger on one side of that and eight on the other, and so on).

But through all those math lessons and the Christian stories we read, I never considered that the gospel might offend some people. In fact, the Bible seemed really . . . nice. That's likely in part because I hadn't yet read any really crazy Old Testament stories, like the one about two bears mauling a bunch of kids for making fun of the prophet Elisha in 2 Kings 2. I think it's also safe to say that from the comfort of my Christian bubble, it didn't occur to me that the things I was learning could ever be considered objectionable to anyone. How could you be offended that the Son of God came to earth, died an awful death, and rose from the grave so we could spend eternity with God? And why would anyone hate Christians for sharing that message?

Ah. The naivety.

I can't go any further without acknowledging that some people hate Christians for good reasons because sometimes we're the worst. When we're smug and unloving, judgmental and self-righteous, Christians are the worst case for Christianity. When we close ranks or treat the church like a museum rather than a hospital, I can understand why the world doesn't like us. When we can't take a joke or spend all of our time pointing out everyone's sin, I don't really want anything to do with us either. But the converse is all the more true. When we're joyful and kind and patient, when we extend the grace to others that Christ afforded us, we are the best case for Christianity. And we're still blazing, bright targets for the hate of the world because of the truth we refuse to deviate from.

> WHEN WE'RE SMUG AND UNLOVING, JUDGMENTAL AND SELF-RIGHTEOUS, CHRISTIANS ARE THE WORST CASE FOR CHRISTIANITY.

The gospel simultaneously is the most inclusive and exclusive message in creation (and I've been kicked out of a few girl gangs, so trust me). It's not inclusive in the buzzword sense. The gospel is inclusive in the truest understanding of the word in that it is for everyone. Literally and exactly everyone. And sometimes I wrestle with that! Have you ever considered that if a terrorist or serial killer accepts Christ and acknowledges Him as their Savior in the final moments of life we'll meet them in heaven? Despite the number of lives they may have taken, if they repent and hand their souls over to Christ, they'll be counted in His number the same way we will be if we belong to Him. (This is proven by Jesus' conversation with the thief on the cross, whom Jesus tells, "Truly, I say to you, today you will be with me in paradise" [Luke 23:43, ESV].) If we're honest, sometimes that can be difficult to stomach because it reduces our acts on earth to what they really are—good deeds that will never get us into heaven.

That, of course, brings us to the reason the gospel is exclusionary. Truth is exclusive in that it rejects everything that's not true. There aren't multiple roads to heaven. "Your truth" isn't the path to a relationship with your Creator. You won't get to heaven by being a good person or helping all the grandmas cross a busy road. You're going to get to heaven because you believed that Jesus Christ died and your sin died with Him. You and I will get to heaven because of the finished work of the Cross, not because of who we are or what we've done.

The gospel is offensive because it shows our complete need for a Savior and total inability to work ourselves into good standing with God. It's my most and least favorite part of Christianity. I love that grace is given through faith, not through my works, so there is nothing I can boast about. I love that it is unearnable, unchangeable, and incapable of being lost or ruined. I love that there is absolutely nothing I can do to make God love me more or love me less.

But at the same time, those inerrant truths rub against my fleshy pride. I want to be able to earn the grace I've been so freely given. I wish my good works affected the overall way in which God sees me. I want to be able to brag about how well I've served the Father so that I can feel better, having put in a little effort. I want to be able to make God love me just a little bit more if I can. But I can't.

That's the whole point. The second you pay someone back for a gift, it ceases to be a gift. If my husband brings home a bouquet and I hand him a twenty-dollar bill, the flowers aren't a gift anymore. And honestly, my offer of money would probably offend him, his sweet gesture reduced to a piece of paper, the thoughtfulness immediately eliminated. But every day we do the same thing with God, trying to give him grubby dollar bills for the most beautiful gift money can buy. All the while He's asking us just to take the flowers. To breathe them in deeply, to enjoy them, to relish them, to know that there was nothing we could have ever done to earn them.

The good news is God doesn't just want to give us allegorical flowers of grace; He's given us everything we need for life and godliness (see 2 Peter 1:3). In our time together we've covered some hard-hitting topics, things we aren't always sure we're allowed to talk about and definitely don't always feel equipped to speak into, but I want to let you in on some insider information: You are qualified. You are because of God's Word imparted to you, alive and applicable even thousands of years later. You are because He gave His Spirit to guide you and help you discern the truth. Every single part of the gospel and of Scripture holds the answers to life's hardest questions. You just need to know what it says, engraining its teachings in your mind, embedding it in your being so that when you react, answer, or engage, what comes out will be the fruit of knowing God so well that He is the One others see.

WISE TO THE WORLD

This life-giving grace is what makes Christians so despised by the world (along with our penchant for being jerks). It's the reason we cannot be friends with the world—because we have been chosen out of it, set apart, not by our own doing but by God's. And yet so many Christians spend their lives trying to make nice with the world. Trying to be liked, accepted, and celebrated by it. We've lost sight of an offensive gospel and have traded it for one that makes us comfortable. Because let me tell you, a comfy gospel doesn't contain Matthew 10:22 and James 4:4:

> You will be hated by everyone because of me, but the one who stands firm to the end will be saved.
>
> MATTHEW 10:22, NIV

> Do you not know that friendship with the world is enmity with God? Therefore whoever wishes to be a friend of the world makes himself an enemy of God.
>
> JAMES 4:4, ESV

Combined, these two verses pack a heck of a one-two punch. One: The world is going to hate you, and two: Being friends with the world makes you an enemy of God. I appreciate that Matthew doesn't beat around the proverbial bush here. He doesn't say "if" or "maybe," he says "you will." You will be hated by everyone because of Jesus is one of the less pretty promises of Scripture. The question is, are you okay with that?

Have you ever wanted to be friends with someone who just plain didn't like you? I have. I've experienced the loss of a once close friendship that I just wasn't ready to let go of yet—even though it was (painfully) obvious that the love they once held in their heart for me had been replaced with disdain. They didn't want me in their life anymore; they thought I was annoying or "too much" and were ready to be rid of me. And instead of taking the hint, I found myself scurrying around trying to pick up the pieces and hand them back to the other person. Giving them gifts for no reason, offering to watch their kids, just trying to be there in hopes it would make them love me again. And it didn't work. They didn't want to be friends with me anymore because their perception of me had changed. Trying to make someone love you hurts. It hurts your pride, it sucks the life out of you, and it sets you up for absolute failure.

This is what happens when you and I try to look like and be loved by the world. It's the same situation. Sure, the world and its voices may not outright tell you they hate you, but Scripture says they will—loud and clear. And then it doubles down, telling you that not only will the world hate you, but that if you spend your time trying to be friends with it, you've made yourself an enemy of God. Because the ways of the world are what put Jesus on the cross. His enemies crucified Him because they knew He wasn't of this world, and they hated the way that made them feel. People don't generally enjoy being faced with the deepest, darkest parts of themselves or their inability to fix themselves (shhh, don't tell self-help culture!). I sure don't.

For example: After encountering the various Enneagram personality types and identifying myself as an 8 (aka "The Challenger"[1]), I read all the worst parts of this number and wanted nothing further to do with any of it. It was quite honestly unenjoyable to read words like *commanding, intense, confrontational* and have to face that I was, in fact, all of those things. I decided it was dumb, pointless, and quite frankly, rude. But once I started to put my pride aside, I realized that God was using this system to reveal some traits in me that I needed to hand over to Him. Obviously, the Enneagram isn't the gospel—I see it as a tool to be used alongside it—but the gospel is even more revealing and offensive to those who have not yet embraced it.

As with everything, there are always Christians who take the idea of exposing others' weaknesses too far. The ones who shame you for knowing every word to a Lil Wayne song or think you'll never enter the gates of heaven if you wear anything but turtlenecks and trousers. The believer who has missed the glory of the Father for the sake of the law. But I think in our day, we're seeing Christians swing further to the other side of the culture versus Christ pendulum.

We're seeing more and more Christians put aside the inerrant truth of the Bible for something that will make people feel all warm and fuzzy inside. Believers are speaking, writing, and sharing opinions as biblical truth, but they are the complete opposite. They don't like that the gospel is inclusive and exclusive. They don't like that it's built on the reality that we need a Savior. They don't like that the Bible calls a spade a spade and offers no apology. But I think more than anything, they don't like that holding fast to biblical truth makes the world hate them. And to a degree, I get it. During my time as an "internet person," I've gained a following mostly thanks to my penchant for rocking the boat. For saying what many people are thinking but are often nervous to say out loud—things like there are two genders or there aren't multiple paths to God or abortion is murder. And every time I've gotten on my platform and talked about things like this that are undebatable, biblical truth (because, yes, I do also talk politics online—but for me those things are always up for debate), I've gotten some of the most hateful messages you can imagine. Like the one saying they hoped my kids would get sick and die. Or the one that told me to kill myself and how to do it. Getting vile, vitriolic messages online (or in real life) never becomes fun. It may get easier, your skin may get thicker, but it's always uncomfortable and sad. The truth is, I don't believe these people hate me. They may think they do, but in the end, they hate the truth of Scripture. Because the truth is often uncomfortable.

If your validation comes from the world applauding your belief system, if you look to places like Hollywood or the mainstream media and find that the majority of voices sound like yours, it may be time to ask yourself some tough questions. Scripture is crystal clear about our purpose and place this side of heaven, and looking like the world simply is not it.

"In the world but not of it" is a popular Christianese phrase that is thrown around in religious settings, but what does it really mean? As a southern Louisiana girl married to an avid fisherman, the analogy of a recreational boat comes to mind. When my husband and I are flying through the waters of the Amite River here in southern Louisiana, our boat is surrounded on all sides by the muddy waters that will eventually feed into Lake Maurepas. The key for a safe journey is that the water stays where it belongs, outside the boat. If we start taking on water, we've got a problem. It's the same with us as children of God living in a broken world. We're here. We're in it and we're supposed to be in the world. It's our job to simultaneously engage the culture around us without allowing it to infiltrate our lives. It's our mission to show up, to build relationships with others, to use our God-given gifts for the Kingdom, to have fun and enjoy the playground called Earth that God has given us. So how do we do that without sacrificing the gospel?

The truth delivered without love is often brutal, but love offered without the truth is enabling. What I want more than anything is the ability to hold truth in one hand and love in the other and offer them to a world desperate for both. The world we're living in is intensely in need of truth. In a time when basically anything can be "your truth" and "facts" are sometimes based more on feelings than reality, people need the truth of the gospel. They need to be set free from the chains of self-saviorism and the lie that what they want is what is best. More than ever our world needs people who love Jesus to step up and boldly proclaim the truth without fear. And they need us to do it because we love them, not because we think they're wrong. Love has to be the thing that drives us to be the hands and feet of Christ, to share His goodness and His glory with a hurting world.

It's time to start telling the truth, friend. Even when it's uncomfortable, even when it would be easier to brush it under the rug, and even when it puts a target on your back. Paul put it perfectly in his letter to the Romans: "For I am not ashamed of the gospel, because it is the power of God that brings salvation to everyone who believes: first to the Jew, then to the Gentile" (Romans 1:16, NIV).

I've never intentionally been ashamed of the gospel, but I've subconsciously made decisions that made it appear like I was. Like the time in college that I completely scrubbed my social media of any mention of church or Jesus because I had a crush on a guy and I wasn't sure how he felt about all that. Cringe city. I wouldn't have told you I was ashamed of the gospel, but I surely wasn't loudly proclaiming it either. Or when I hedge my bets on speaking the truth of Scripture when around new people so they don't find me controversial or argumentative. It may not be Peter pre-Crucifixion level denouncement, but shame has held me back from being bold about the power of God to bring salvation. And who knows what God could have done with my obedience in any of those situations? What if that guy I liked had been on the cusp of entering into a relationship with God and knowing he could talk to me about it would've been the push he needed? Or what if a new acquaintance needed a little help telling the truth when they disagreed with what was being discussed, and I could've given it to them?

In the end, I think the problem is that you and I sometimes lose sight of eternity. We trade the glory that eternity holds for momentary and fleeting approval of people on earth. We want to be liked more than to share the potentially lifesaving power of the gospel with others. So we water it down. We tweak our words so we won't be canceled. We make them more consumable so they'll buy our books or listen to our podcasts. And along the way, we miss it. We miss the chance to live this life unashamed of the gospel, with our eyes set on Jesus, full steam ahead to complete the mission set before us.

There isn't a five-step formula to being bolder in your proclamation of Christ. There's no to-do list, no workbook. There is simply the knock-you-off-your-feet glory of God and the truth that His power and majesty are all you need to move forward. To make you brave. To give you the words. You are Moses, and this is your burning bush. God doesn't mind that you're not the most eloquent of the lot. He's not concerned if you're slow to speak or if you worry about what people think of you. He doesn't need you to be gifted in one particular way in order to use you. No matter what your rebuttal is, this is the Lord's answer: "Who gave human beings their mouths? Who makes them deaf or mute? Who gives them sight or makes them blind? Is it not I, the LORD? Now go; I will help you speak and will teach you what to say" (Exodus 4:11-12, NIV).

Today is your Egypt, friend. All around you there are slaves waiting to be set free by the truth you hold in your heart. The truth of the Bible. The truth that offends and sets free. The truth that we can't do it all on our own, that we need a Savior and He has already come. There are people around you waiting to be plucked out of lives of sin by the loving truth that the Father made them for more than the lives they're living. There are hearts needing to hear that they are not enough to save themselves, but that the One who came to save them will make them enough. Mothers, fathers, daughters, sons, brothers, and sisters are waiting, their hearts parched, dry land in need of the Living Water. And God has specifically designed you to set them free in a way only you can do. In a way I could never do. He has perfectly pieced you and your life together for this moment: to go be Moses to those desperate for the truth spoken in love.

So go set them free.

ACKNOWLEDGMENTS

To Jeremy, without whom none of this would exist—thank you. Thank you for being the unicorn husband that you are, for always supporting my craziest dreams, for inspiring me and always bringing me back to the Cross.

To my girls, Pacey and Elliot, this book is for you and all the girls like you who will change the world one day. My hope is that by breaking the confining mold created by modern Christianity, you're free to be exactly who God created you to be as you grow into women of God. Thanks for loving and giving Mommy grace when I was a complete crazy person during the writing of this book.

To Kara, the woman who plucked me out of obscurity and saw the potential for a killer book, who held my hand the entire way, put up with temper tantrums and meltdowns and untimely phone calls—thank you for believing in me and being my champion.

DISCUSSION QUESTIONS

INTRODUCTION: WHY I CHOSE A CRAPPY— NOT A CURATED—FAITH

1. When it comes to your life or your faith, in what ways have you tried to curate—to be selective about—what others see? What are the benefits of doing so? The drawbacks?

2. What do you think of when you hear the term "crappy Christian"? How, if at all, might you apply that term to yourself?

CHAPTER 1: WHAT AM I CHASING?

1. Have you ever chased something—a relationship, a job, a business—only to realize that it didn't deliver what you expected? Explain.

2. Near the end of the chapter, Blake lists the three questions she asks herself to keep her motives in check: Whose glory am I working for? Which of my relationships is most important to me? How am I using my time? Consider how you spend your days, and then answer these questions for yourself. What do the answers tell you about what you are chasing?

CHAPTER 2: WHERE DO I GET MY WORTH?

1. Does "hustle culture" appeal to you? Why or why not?

2. Which of the Scripture passages Blake provides (see especially page 26) most motivates you to live for Christ and His Kingdom?

CHAPTER 3: CAN GOD REALLY USE MY WEAKNESSES?

1. When confronted with a personal weakness, how do you respond? Do you strike back, try to hide, or do something else?

2. Have you ever asked God to remove a particularly hard struggle or burden? What was His response?

CHAPTER 4: WHAT DO I DO WHEN MY DREAMS ARE DASHED?

1. What dream have you had dashed? Looking back, can you see how God used that for your good? Explain.

2. When God asks you to do something difficult, are you more likely to respond with the anxiety of Moses ("No, LORD, don't send me") or the faithful trust of Jeremiah ("'For I know the plans I have for you,' declares the LORD")?

CHAPTER 5: SHOULD I FOLLOW MY FEELINGS OR THE TRUTH?

1. Are you more likely to allow your feelings or facts to drive your actions and reactions? What are the benefits and drawbacks to living this way?

2. Blake suggests that God's grace enables us to live informed by our feelings but defined by the truth of His love for us.

How would your life be different if you lived from that understanding?

CHAPTER 6: WHY DO I ALWAYS FEEL LIKE TOO MUCH OR NEVER ENOUGH?

1. How familiar were you with the Proverbs 31 woman before reading this chapter? How has your understanding of her changed?

2. Have you ever been made to feel as if you don't have all the required attributes to be called a virtuous and capable woman? Explain.

CHAPTER 7: WHAT'S IN IT (THE BIBLE) FOR ME?

1. Blake says that "being steeped in Scripture is the most effective way to take your thoughts captive" (page 84). Do you agree? Why and how does that work?

2. On pages 85–87, Blake discusses two common reasons people don't read their Bibles. Do you identify with either? If not, can you name another reason why you may not turn to Scripture?

CHAPTER 8: WOULD JESUS BE A JERK?

1. What drew many people to Jesus during His time on earth? What repelled others?

2. How do you think we can balance the need to speak both truth and love to others? Who have you seen do that well?

CHAPTER 9: WHY DOES IT TAKE SO LONG TO HEAL?

1. Following her daughter's brush with death, Blake describes how she looked okay on the outside but felt as if she were falling apart on the inside. What factors contributed to that? Can you relate to that experience in any way?

2. Blake says a primary reason healing often takes longer than it has to is because "we don't start at the root." If you are struggling with a long-held trauma, can you trace your pain back to a wound or false belief? If so, describe.

CHAPTER 10: WHY AM I SO DANG TIRED?

1. Describe a situation in which you stopped prioritizing rest because you felt the results of a project or situation were all up to you.

2. Which of the seven types of rest (physical, mental, sensory, creative, emotional, social, and spiritual) do you currently need most? What is one thing you can do today or tomorrow to practice that type of rest?

CHAPTER 11: MY CHURCH HURT ME; NOW WHAT?

1. In what ways, if any, have you been hurt by a church?

2. After reading this chapter, what step could you take either to process your own hurt or to help someone you know who has been hurt by a faith community?

CHAPTER 12: WHY ARE CHRISTIANS SO WEIRD ABOUT SEX?

1. How does what you were taught about sex as a teenager affect your view of sexuality now?

2. What would you say the church gets right and wrong about sex?

CHAPTER 13: WHY DO FRIENDSHIP BREAKUPS HURT SO MUCH?

1. Consider a friendship breakup that still fills you with regret or a sense of loss. What led to the loss of this relationship? What did this chapter teach you about how you might process that loss?

2. When a friend hurts you, are you more likely to cut them off completely or do everything possible to maintain the friendship? How might you respond to such situations in a healthier way?

CHAPTER 14: SHOULD I JUST FAKE FORGIVENESS?

1. Can you relate to Blake's definition of fake forgiveness? If so, recall a situation in your life where this was your response. How well did that serve you?

2. If you are still stinging from the way someone hurt you, would you say you are at the point where you most need to acknowledge, forgive, or shed the weight you've been carrying? What action could you take today to begin that process?

CHAPTER 15: WHY DOES THE GOSPEL MAKE ME UNCOMFORTABLE?

1. Do you think Christians today are more likely to err on the side of being smug and judgmental or vacillating and permissive when discussing the gospel? Explain.

2. Blake challenges us this way: "It's time to start telling the truth, friend." As you finish this book and consider the many questions raised in each chapter, where do you feel called and better enabled to speak the truth in love?

NOTES

CHAPTER 1 WHAT AM I CHASING?

1. C. S. Lewis, *Mere Christianity* (New York: HarperOne, 2001), 136–37.

CHAPTER 2 WHERE DO I GET MY WORTH?

1. See, for example, Ephesians 5:15-17; Philippians 2:14-15; 1 Timothy 5:8; and 2 Timothy 2:15.

CHAPTER 3 CAN GOD REALLY USE MY WEAKNESSES?

1. If you think Indiana Jones lived an adventurous and dangerous life, see the apostle Paul's list of experiences in 2 Corinthians 11:16-33.
2. Enduring Word, "2 Corinthians 12—The Strength of Grace in Weakness," https://enduringword.com/bible-commentary/2-corinthians-12/.

CHAPTER 4 WHAT DO I DO WHEN MY DREAMS ARE DASHED?

1. *Merriam-Webster*, s.v. "failure," accessed October 14, 2021, https://www.merriam-webster.com/dictionary/failure.

CHAPTER 8 WOULD JESUS BE A JERK?

1. See, for example, 1 Timothy 1:3-7; 1 Timothy 4:1-2; 1 Timothy 6:3-5; 2 Timothy 1:13-14; 2 Timothy 2:23-26; 2 Timothy 4:2-5.

CHAPTER 9 WHY DOES IT TAKE SO LONG TO HEAL?

1. "Facts and Statistics," Anxiety & Depression Association of America, accessed October 25, 2021, https://adaa.org/understanding-anxiety/facts-statistics.
2. For more on Paul's arrests, see Acts 16:19-23; 22:23-30; and 2 Timothy 2:9. In 2 Corinthians 11:23-28, Paul offers an extensive list of the many ways he has suffered for Christ.

CHAPTER 12 WHY ARE CHRISTIANS SO WEIRD ABOUT SEX?

1. Steven C. Martino et al., "Virginity Pledges among the Willing: Delays in First Intercourse and Consistency of Condom Use," *Journal of Adolescent Health* 43, no. 4 (October 2008): 341–48, https://pubmed.ncbi.nlm.nih .gov/18809131/.
2. Janet Elise Rosenbaum, "Patient Teenagers? A Comparison of the Sexual Behavior of Virginity Pledgers and Matched Nonpledgers," *Pediatrics* 123, no. 1 (January 2009): 110–20, https://pubmed.ncbi.nlm.nih.gov /19117832/.

CHAPTER 13 WHY DO FRIENDSHIP BREAKUPS HURT SO MUCH?

1. Dharius Daniels, "Who's at Your Table?" Change Church, January 5, 2020, https://lifechange.org/sermons/whos-at-your-table/.
2. Casey Beathard and Edward Monroe Hill, "Find Out Who Your Friends Are," Sony/ATV Songs LLC, Lavender Zoo Music, Careers-BMG Music Publishing and Sagrabeaux Songs, 2007.

CHAPTER 14 SHOULD I JUST FAKE FORGIVENESS?

1. *Strong's Greek Concordance*, s.v. *phortizó*, https://biblehub.com/greek/5412 .htm.

CHAPTER 15 WHY DOES THE GOSPEL MAKE ME UNCOMFORTABLE?

1. Ian Morgan Cron, *The Road Back to You* (Downers Grove, IL: IVP Press, 2016), 26.

ABOUT THE AUTHOR

Blake Guichet is a writer, rebel, and founder of the Crappy Christian Co., which aims to teach women how to use their God-given gifts for the Kingdom. She is the host of the hit podcast *Confessions of a Crappy Christian*—a weekly show that specializes in conversations with guests about their passions, struggles, and all the things they aren't sure they can talk about. A proud Enneagram 8, American history buff, and playlist enthusiast, Blake's primary goal in all aspects of her ministry is to tell the truth while always pointing people to Jesus. Visit her online at crappychristianco.com.

JOIN THE CRAPPY CHRISTIAN CO.

helping you be wild + brave + free

find community, growth and freedom
through groups, courses and coaching.

crappychristianco.com

CP1797